CULTIVATE COMMUNITY

CULTIVATE COMMUNITY

ASHLEY LIN

NEW DEGREE PRESS

CULTIVATE COMMUNITY

ISBN   978-1-63676-459-7   *Paperback*

           978-1-63676-460-3   *Kindle Ebook*

           978-1-63676-461-0   *Ebook*

CONTENTS

———

INTRODUCTION

———

Most of my closest friends are people I've met in online communities.

If you told me that would happen two years ago, I probably wouldn't have believed you either. Here's what happened:

Throughout 2019, I was part of more than twenty Slack workspaces for various clubs, teams, programs, and other groups I was involved in. Slack describes itself as a "channel-based messaging platform designed to help teams work together more effectively." For many of the groups I belonged to, from nationwide fellowships to start-up incubator programs, Slack became the go-to platform to introduce an online community component to their work.

Online communities seemed like a great idea. The physical connections these programs offered were life changing for me. What more could I want than a digital space to preserve my learnings and stay in touch with incredible humans I felt inspired and energized by?

It turns out execution was a bit harder than expected.

Everyone wanted to "stay connected," but in Slack, no one really posted anything. The love and energy that marked our in-person convenings just didn't translate well online. "Happy birthdays!" would rush in when it was someone's turn to become a year older, conversation would spike for a day, and it would largely return to crickets for the rest of the week. Regardless of whether we tried Slack or Instagram group chats, the vibe was largely still the same.

I quickly became disenchanted with online communities. They didn't seem to work, much less capture the magic of community that happened in person. It was just harder to create deep care, a sense of belonging, and real agency through screens on a digital device.

Thus, when I was selected to join the Civics Unplugged Fellowship and their Slack channel in January 2020, I wasn't expecting much at all. I was blown away by what I found.

* * *

Civics Unplugged (CU) is a nonpartisan 501c3 social enterprise whose mission is to empower the leaders of Generation Z to build a brighter future for humanity. I was a part of the inaugural cohort of the CU Fellowship: a free, virtual, three-month leadership program that prepares thousands of high school students each year in the fundamentals of personal development, systems thinking, and civic literacy.

When I saw *"Join our Slack channel!"* as one of the onboarding tasks, I honestly thought it would be just another Slack workspace that I joined, introduced myself in, and never checked again.

To my surprise, within the first few minutes of scrolling through CU's Slack, I was smiling. There was such a fun and open Gen Z vibe forming around civics. The #general channel was bursting with memes, photos, and emojis. The back-and-forth banter and community jokes created a space in which I felt like there was a real possibility of getting to know people beyond the rigid "Hi, I'm *name* and my accomplishments are *x*, *y*, *z*."

I remember posting my introduction in Slack, which didn't feature my LinkedIn profile or the organizations I ran, but rather a simple name, age, location, and an agreement with someone else about the need to send tacos to elected officials. In response, I received a bunch of heart emojis, some Ben Franklin emojis (a custom one added by a CU Fellow), and a couple of "Welcome!" messages.

Within the first few hours, a fellow even called CU's Slack "the civics party."

It's crucial to realize this space didn't magically form. The people at CU didn't just start a Slack channel, drop people in it, and assume they would click and a community would form. It was much more intentional. For example, clear directions were shared on why and how I might use tacos (digital tokens of appreciation) to shout out fellow community members. A ritual of morning reflection threads was created, which encouraged members to open up, share their thoughts, and reflect on topics relevant to the community's purpose. Even CU's cofounders were active on Slack, welcoming members, sparking conversations, and facilitating connections.

Fast forward six months when the fellowship ended, the community did not.

Graduates of the fellowship, called Builders, went on to launch Civics 2030, a ten-year campaign to build a movement of young people who want to ensure humanity is headed in the right direction. Builders have organized a virtual CU Summer Camp, launched a campaign for open primaries, and created a diversity and inclusion training program.

Through CU, I have found my inner circle of friends. These are people I consult on everything from how to unplug from extracurriculars to how I value my time. We've worked on projects together that gave me so much hope I cried happy tears. They've kept me anchored during times where I felt like the community and my life were falling apart. I know I can count on these people to stick with me through the ups and downs, and that no matter what happens, we'd find a way to take care of each other and create positive impact together.

CU has shown me how digital-first communities *can* work and put each of us on an upward trajectory.

* * *

Flourishing digital communities are no longer just a nice-to-have.

We live in an age of not just increasing digitization, but also increasing loneliness and mental illness. Adults lament about young people spending so much time on digital devices and believe social media is to blame for our disconnection. But what if our devices are portals to smaller, more intimate digital spaces that inspire us to become the best versions of ourselves? What if digital communities keep us connected and moving forward in a time when the forces of society, from pandemics to the attention economy, seem to keep us apart?

Beyond helping us find our inner circle of friends, digital communities help us coordinate with people different from us in order to tackle today's critical global issues. As the activists behind #FridaysForFuture and March For Our Lives have shown us, digital public spaces like subreddits and Twitter threads are key building blocks of bottom-up power.

Digital-first communities allow their members to experience something we could all use more of: what it feels like to be truly seen, understood, and included. When people have the opportunity to experience this on a small scale, we gain agency to replicate these spaces in our families, communities, and the world.

That's why beyond being part of incredible communities like Civics Unplugged, I've also created ones of my own. I've founded organizations like Project Exchange, a youth-led 501c3 nonprofit democratizing access to study abroad. Every cohort, we welcome hundreds of students from over thirty countries into an online cultural exchange community, where they're matched with peer accountability partners, placed in "host families," and participate in everything from potlucks to world fairs. Digital communities are an avenue to help people get together, take care of each other, and harness our imagination to create the world we want to see.

Our world needs more community builders. This is where you come in.

* * *

This book was created to demystify the "magic" behind creating flourishing online communities.

It's for anyone who wants to learn more about how to build your own digital communities or make an existing group more community-like. It's for social changemakers, activists, and organizers who want to figure out how to build power in people online and catalyze change. It's for anyone trying to figure out how to keep their community connected and thriving in an increasingly digital world.

The book serves as a practical how-to guide on what exactly a digital-first community is and how to create one. Part 1 offers a historical perspective on community: what community means, the rise of digital communities, and societal trends converging to make digital-first community building more important than ever. Part 2 is more technically instructive and explains how to create the structures, practices, and cultures shared by the most successful communities. You'll examine the steps of community building through the metaphor of a garden and provocations like "lead with love" and "decentralize power." Finally, Part 3 helps you apply these concepts in your own communities and the real world.

Digital-first community building isn't easy. It requires time, energy, and hard work, but it doesn't have to be a paralyzing process either. Being a space-maker and community builder is a joy practice. We all deserve to know how to create the spaces we need and want to see. Let this book be your guide.

If you're ready to strengthen the digital communities you belong to or start new ones, read on!

1.1

DEFINITION OF COMMUNITY

"Some people think they are in community, but they are only in proximity. True community requires commitment and openness. It is a willingness to extend yourself to encounter and know the other."

—DAVID SPANGLER

Like many young people, I've spent most of my life trying to figure out where I belong, how I contribute, and why it all matters. I didn't realize there was a term associated with the things I was looking for: community.

Merriam-Webster defines community as "people with common interests living in a particular area." Growing up, I closely followed this definition and thought community was people who lived close to me—a belief reinforced through my exposure to local *community* service activities such as picking up trash on nearby hiking trails, planting trees in city parks, and delivering meals for seniors in the neighborhood.

As I was having conversations while making this book, one student I spoke with asked, "What even is community building? Is it like building houses?"

This mindset isn't uncommon—and if it's where you're at right now, you're not alone. Community seems like it's used to describe all sorts of things. It's a pretty word, but also pretty vague and sometimes just plain confusing. It's also hard because as you see above, community means different things to different people.

Here's my understanding of community: **a group of people who build power together through belonging and mutual care.**

Using this definition, I'll show you community is more than a plot of land or building houses. It's even more than a group of people with a common goal or shared identity. Digital technologies change what it means to be local and allow us to connect whenever, wherever, with people and experiences previously out of reach. It is critical for us to expand the meaning of community, in order to tap into its full potential to bring people together and help them achieve much more than they would've been able to alone.

* * *

It's an understatement to say my personal definition of community has evolved over time, as I'm sure yours have as well.

My own definition started to shift from **people who live close to me** to **people who look like me** in middle school. I'd always attended Sunday Chinese School, and as a child, hung out a lot with my parents' friends—who also happened to be Taiwanese immigrants. Naturally, in sixth grade when I had to find people to sit with at lunch, I gravitated toward others who looked like me.

In high school, community became **people who did things with me**. My high school has over 2,000 students and over thirty clubs and organizations on campus. In ninth grade, I signed up for everything: STEM Club, Key Club, Interact Club, Future Business Leaders of America, and more. I started feeling a lot more connected to fellow club members than "other Taiwanese immigrants in Vancouver, WA." Participation in school clubs prompted me to realize a community isn't just a collection of people with a common geographical location or cultural identity. Deeper forces are at work to create a sense of belonging, which doesn't just magically appear; people have to do things together. Through club meetings, service projects, pizza parties, and more, the practices we engage in spark connections of trust and care.

During my junior year of high school, my definition of community changed yet again: **the group of people I invite into my life**. Up until this point, I largely believed communities could only form in-real-life. But during junior year, I wasn't at school much due to traveling for meetings and conferences. As a result, I stepped back from a lot of school clubs and the communities I had found within them. It wasn't a surprise the sense of closeness I felt rapidly deteriorated. After all, I wasn't seeing people in person every day anymore.

What *did* surprise me is how I was able to find other communities online to fill the gaps without ever having in-real-life club meetings and pizza parties.

I joined #BuiltByGirls, a Slack community of over 2,000 female and non-binary young people interested in careers in tech and social impact. I found myself spending hours in the #girls-building-now and #you-glow-girl channels, where I was able to support and team up with people—something I previously believed could only be done in-person. When I was intentional about caring for others, even online, I was able to recreate intimate community.

This revelation was exciting to me. Suddenly, I could belong to so many more communities! My experience greatly contrasted the traditional definition of community as a plot of land.

Finally, the most recent shift in my perception of community came in March 2020. To be honest, I didn't think much about community before COVID-19. Did you? For many of us, community was always there, something that kind of just happened. In-person connections of convenience, from bumping into people in hallways to spontaneous conversations at lunch, allowed us to get to know each other and facilitated deeper relationships over time. Where community bloomed, it was beautiful. Where it didn't form... no biggie, right? We can suck it up and make it through a lifeless club meeting or two.

But COVID made me realize it *was* a biggie, and we can't afford to cross our fingers and hope community magically forms on its own—especially online, where it's even more unlikely to happen. Online communities are completely opt-in, and because people aren't required to be in them like school or work, it's impossible for communities to accidentally blossom. Furthermore, social distancing exacerbated difficult emotions people grapple with, like feeling lonely, out of place, or ignored. The pandemic made it impossible to continue pushing these feelings under the rug. Instead, it called for new digital community structures and processes that helped us become aware of what the people around us are going through.

We could no longer ignore the importance and significance of being part of flourishing communities. And community isn't just about the well-being of individuals. Many of them exist to tackle real problems and injustices. But how can we make an impact when every community member is not adequately cared for and supported? How can we make the world a better place if our own community isn't flourishing?

Community building starts with creating a culture where every community member feels connected, supported, and empowered. In the process of helping people discover and hone their gifts, we realize community building is about building power in people. It's showing that by pooling together our resources and making decisions together, we can take care of each other and the world around us.

Dustin Liu, the ninth Youth Observer to the United Nations, once told me, "A community that's very strong for me is one where I can bring my full self. Making people feel special, making people feel seen, and making people feel heard is just so crucial." Communities should help people feel as though they are growing with each other into the best versions of themselves. By doing so, positive communities help people realize their full potential and be of service to the world.

This is the arc that shaped my understanding of community: people who live close to me → people who look like me → people who do things with me → people I invite into my life → people who make me feel powerful through a sense of belonging and mutual care.

Whereas my definition of community used to be limited by geography and identity, I've realized community is about caring spaces that enable me to grow into my authentic self.

* * *

Interestingly, this definition forces us to realize many of the "communities" we belong to are less community-like than we expect.

Ruqaiyah Angeles is a Muslim Filipino woman and a computer science student at San Francisco State University, passionate about increasing representation within the tech industry. She recognized early on the importance of community between people of color, women-identifying folks, and other marginalized people in STEAM. As a result, Ruqaiyah relentlessly searched for spaces where she could meet like-minded people with similar aspirations and vision for the future.

When I first came across Ruqaiyah's LinkedIn profile, I was intrigued by the sheer number of online communities she belonged to. In her search for belonging and solidarity as an underrepresented person in the tech space, Ruqaiyah had amassed a number of roles—almost all of which had the word "community" somewhere in the title or job description.

I could see why Ruqaiyah found these organizations so attractive. They had bold visions, such as "to connect, inspire, and empower girls in STEAM" and "to build wealth and prosperity in diverse communities through jobs in technology." It seemed these were places where she could find her people. By calling the group a "community," these organizations promised care and belonging—something many weren't prepared to offer.

This became clear within the first few minutes of my conversation with Ruqaiyah, who described one of the organizations: "As far as virtual community goes, it's very one-sided. They kind of lecture, lecture, lecture, talk, talk, talk. It's not necessarily a collaborative thing. During meetings and other big events, the community is very dictatorship-like."

This completely blew my mind. It confused me how community and dictatorship could describe the same organization and how community could ever be a one-sided thing. Why did Ruqaiyah feel like this was a community? It was the idea people with a common interest came together in one place—online. This understanding was similar to what I thought community meant before I experienced the connection that comes from doing meaningful things together. Ruqaiyah reached a similar conclusion: Just because people are in one place, associate with the same identity group, or label themselves a "community," it doesn't mean connections magically emerge. Connections on a deeper level require work, no matter how many "things in common" people start out with.

From a marketing perspective, "community" is sometimes substituted for groups with demographic similarities. Fabian Pfortmüller is the founder and CEO of the Together Institute, an organization dedicated to building healthy, caring, and impactful communities. He notes "the term 'community' is really hot in the sales, marketing, and events spaces, because it alludes to more than just a transactional customer-company relationship." Tacking on the community label to products and experiences provides a sense of cohesion and good intention.

The term community is similarly hot in the youth changemaking space because it alludes to more than just a transactional student-organization relationship. In a world where students often start organizations for clout, calling something a community softens and adds a positive connotation. You can even see this phenomenon in how we describe our schools: I'm not just a student; I'm part of the *learning community* at Union High School. See how that leveled it up?

Fabian believes when most people say "community," they mean "a series of monthly events, a Facebook page, a group of customers that has loyalty toward a specific brand, a yearly conference, all social media followers, everyone who uses Twitter, people who happen to vote the same way." The incorrect use of community has immense repercussions. We end up promising things we can't provide, which leaves community members feeling disillusioned by the idea and even a bit betrayed. The more we use it incorrectly, the more "community" loses its meaning.

In the case of most youth-led nonprofits, clubs, and friend groups, this deceit isn't intentional. Most people want to do good, but simply don't know how to create spaces of belonging and power, or what structures and practices they can adopt to do so. As a result, many groups and organizations never become true communities and realize their full potential.

Ruqaiyah told me about a few more "communities" she was a part of: "It's very much run by the people who started it. Everyone else kind of jumps in and out whenever they want to." For another one, she said, "It's a community as far as everybody's down to support and help out and be a part of things… but we don't talk to each other really." Almost as an afterthought, Ruqaiyah asked, "Does that make sense?"

She paused a bit, and with a slight shake of her head, answered her own question. Communities can't form if people don't even talk to each other.

* * *

There is a growing problem where we call things communities, even when they're not. Part of it is a simple misunderstanding of what community is. I've spoken with dozens of people in quasi-communities, who share it's hard to know whether you've discovered a real community if you haven't personally experienced one before. Instead, anything that involves shared identity is now a community, even if it doesn't cultivate a sense of belonging or collective power.

This begs the question: What do thriving digital communities look like? How do we create them?

Before we dive into the step-by-step "how to build community" section, I want to share two different stories of people who have redefined community and created the online spaces they need. We'll explore the themes in these stories—creating space, giving people real power, small experiments to foster community spirit—in later chapters. For now, let these stories spark your questions and ideas about how the different components all fit together.

First, the rest of Ruqaiyah's story.

As she continued traversing various youth-led "communities," Ruqaiyah noticed the biggest pitfall was these groups focus too much on everything they're supposed to do.

Ruqaiyah explains we know our team members based on their role and how they contribute to the community, but nothing beyond that, which is why community doesn't form. "I'm tired of not knowing your favorite color, what school you go to, or basic things that are a part of you," Ruqaiyah said. "But we don't know, because all we talk about is what our next steps within this organization are, when the next workshop is coming out, and things like that."

Frustrated that she couldn't find the connections she craved, Ruqaiyah decided to start Breaking Barriers, a youth-led organization that assists women and people of color breaking into tech through meaningful relationships with each other. These relationships laid the foundation for knowledge, resources, and other forms of support to be circulated among members.

"We want people to break the barrier of being shy, quiet, and afraid to share knowledge and ask for help," said Ruqaiyah.

In prior experiences, Ruqaiyah experienced how dreadful it was to get people to do things without relationships with one another. As a result, creating space for informal relationships to emerge was at the center of Breaking Barriers. Through spontaneous hangouts, movie nights, and late-night text message chats about everything from COVID to mental health, community members were no longer just "another person working on x project." They were her friends.

When I asked Ruqaiyah the key ingredient to build community, her answer was simple: willingness. The biggest barrier is not that people aren't the same (in geographic location, cultural identity, or something else), but that they aren't willing or *able* to be vulnerable with others. Especially in hierarchical structures that lack meaningful relationships, people are less willing to put themselves out there for fear they won't be accepted.

This was when I realized the symbolism behind Breaking Barriers' name is two-fold: to break barriers for women in STEAM, and also to break barriers about what it means to be in a group of people working toward shared goals. Leadership doesn't need to be rigid to be competent. Compassion and high standards are not mutually exclusive. There's a lot of untapped potential when group members don't learn about each other as friends.

Ruqaiyah's journey shows us we might not be able to *find* the communities we are looking for. Maybe they don't exist. In these scenarios, it's up to us to step up and *create* these spaces for ourselves and others. By starting Breaking Barriers, Ruqaiyah was able to design the community she wanted from the ground up and embed community-like practices into its design.

After years of chasing community, starting Breaking Barriers was how Ruqaiyah finally found her own.

* * *

That said, starting something new is not the only way. I'm not trying to convince you to leave your clubs and organizations that aren't community-like; in fact, quite the opposite. In addition to creating your own, I hope this book gives you the tools you need to shift culture in existing groups. Imagine if your current extracurricular activities could feel like real communities…

Shivali Gulati, a rising freshman at UC Santa Cruz, knows that feeling.

Similar to Ruqaiyah, Shivali recognizes the importance of community to reach shared goals. In high school, she founded Girl Genius, a nonprofit that creates an inclusive community for women and non-binary people of color in STEAM. Girl Genius organizes a quarterly e-magazine and hosts frequent social media takeovers featuring relatable and inspiring female changemakers.

Girl Genius first popped on my radar when they became one of the first youth-led organizations to host consistent weekly Instagram takeovers (which they've now hosted more than one hundred of!). Not only has Girl Genius built a robust social media following, they also launched an intimate Slack community in 2020. It's now 3,700 members strong and constantly growing. Their Slack features everything from a popping #ask-me-anything channel with accomplished founders, to #all-smiles-here, featuring positive quotes, memes, and other community bonding content.

A lot of youth-led nonprofits started forming Slack communities in March 2020 as a result of the pandemic—many of which were incredibly disappointing, the "not-quite communities" discussed above. At first, I thought Girl Genius was one of the organizations who jumped on the bandwagon. I didn't have high expectations, but when I joined and experienced the joyful, engaged community firsthand, I knew I had to learn more about how it started.

Back in 2018, Shivali pitched the idea of a Slack community during the debriefing call for issue one of Girl Genius' e-magazine. Instead, her directors suggested they should focus on team bonding first, learn how to navigate that, and then apply those insights to a larger, public group. Girl Genius recognized community isn't just about getting a group of people with shared identity and goals in the same room. Fostering connections between them requires time, intention, and skill.

For the next year, Shivali and her team explored what it truly means to be in community. In the typical youth-led nonprofit "community," organizational structure is very top down. It's easy to feel like you're just given an assignment every Friday. "How can we create a place where someone can voice both positive and negative things that happened to them and have open discussions about it," Shivali asked.

With awareness and maturity, the Girl Genius team realized they weren't quite ready to start a community yet. Community spirit needs to start at the smallest levels and expand outwards, from within internal leadership to the organization as a whole. Shivali notes in youth-led nonprofits, your group's leaders are also your most engaged members and target audience. If you aren't able to build community within the team, you can't expect to do it on a larger scale. Scaling something that doesn't exist is a recipe for disaster. So, they experimented. Shivali created a team bonding channel in which she posted a daily question and asked team members to spend fifteen minutes reading what others shared and crafting their own response. Without team bonding, certain people might've never met each other because they were working on different projects. Intentional structures for meeting folks and getting to know each other planted the seeds for care and collaboration.

Another key step Girl Genius took was starting Week 0, a team-bonding-only week before any assignments are given (the Girl Genius team works in four-month chunks, which follows their e-magazine production cycle). "A lot of organizations are like, 'Post an intro when you join the team' and that's it," said Shivali. "We spend a week before work starts playing Skribbl.io and just talking about life, because we are dedicated to getting to know you as a human being." Week 0 not only tells, but shows new Girl Genius team members community is a core value.

Remember, all of this learning came *before* Girl Genius launched their thriving public Slack community.

So, if you're looking at our definition of community and feeling like most of the groups you belong to—clubs, families, friend groups—are missing the mark, it's not the end of the world. You can do what Ruqaiyah did and start a flourishing digital-first community of your own or take inspiration from Shivali and help your group become more community-like.

Create space for informal relationships to take root. Give people ownership over community structure and culture.

Recognizing the importance of community spirit and committing to cultivate it within your internal leadership is the first step.

* * *

If you still think community is a natural result of geographic location or shared identity, think again.

In addition to having something in common, flourishing digital communities require trust. Both Ruqaiyah and Shivali have cultivated a team culture where individuals feel like they can create informal, *real* connections with others. Members have a voice in the decision-making process and creative control over where the organization is headed.

Building trust between members can be as simple as daily reflection threads, where people pose thoughtful questions to each other. It can be intensive cohort-based experiences, like a small discussion and mutual support group. Think about communities as "relationship gyms," where people can opt into tons of different experiences to cultivate their relationship muscle—the muscle that holds the community together.

Ultimately, if you've been in pseudo "communities" before, you'll need to unlearn the expectations you've developed. The promise of community is so much more: to be truly seen and understood, to feel cared for and like you belong, and to have real power to change the world with those around you.

We all deserve communities that allow us to gain agency and self-sufficiency. We all deserve spaces that facilitate our flourishing. I hope this book reveals your power to cultivate these spaces.

1.2

EVOLUTION OF DIGITAL COMMUNITIES

"If Facebook is people you know talking about things you don't care about, then Reddit is people you don't know talking about things you do care about."

—ZUBAIR JANALI,

As you know, "community" is much more than a neighborhood or geographic location. In an increasingly digital world, community encompasses not just in-person clubs and organizations, but all sorts of internet groups.

Gen Z, the generation born after 1996, are digital natives who've grown up in the era of social media. We've always been able to connect through our devices. According to a report from the GlobalWebIndex, young people ages sixteen to twenty-four spent an average of seven hours per day online in 2019.

There's a reason why Gen Z spends so much time online: we're searching for digital communities that meet needs many of our in-person communities cannot. We're searching for spaces in which we can make true friends and be our authentic selves. We're looking to find our next co-founders and teammates. We're hoping to learn from and work with people who are geographically, culturally, and ideologically different from us to create positive change in the world.

Given the sheer amount of time Gen Z spends online, it's no surprise Gen Zers seek higher quality, intimate digital communities that reflect our values. So, what does the future of powerful digital-first communities look like?

* * *

In order to understand where digital communities are heading, we have to first understand where they started.

Back in 1969, the internet as we know it was created as ARPAnet. Ethan Zuckerman, a professor of public policy, communication, and information at the University of Massachusetts, explains the 1970s saw new digital tools that would inspire many of the community-building technologies we use today. For example, the first mailing lists, bulletin boards, chat technology, webpages, and collaborative wikis were created during this period.

At first, these tools were sparse due to the small number of people with access to devices and the internet. It was difficult to find a message board or chat room with an active user base aligned with your interests, which made finding a good one feel even more special and important. Slowly, handfuls of people started gathering online, holding discussions, and using bulletin boards—web pages dedicated to a certain topic where users could post messages and respond to others. People were able to interact with others in an entirely new way. User-experience designer Josh Higgins writes about the 1970s internet, "On my favorite communities we could name almost every user, we knew when each other logged on, we got worried when we didn't see someone online like they usually were... Not only could we get into deep nerdy discussions about the interest the forum was built around, but we could also get into deep discussions about each other's lives." It became clear digital spaces have the potential to create intimate connections mirroring the ones we discover in person.

As more people got online, small mailing lists and hidden bulletin boards gave rise to bigger forums. Multi-leveled communication and governance structures were created to support the increasing number of people who joined. The sense of camaraderie and deep knowledge of others, such as what Josh experienced, grew among frequent visitors.

In this way, the first digital communities bloomed.

* * *

Since then, the popularity and use cases of digital communities have skyrocketed. As our world becomes more interconnected, we must coordinate with people who are different from us to tackle global issues. Digital communities enable us to team up with people who we otherwise might have never met and contribute to our collective well-being.

Four patterns have shaped digital communities thus far: social networks, crowdsourcing, curation, and online organizing.

Social Networks

The first social networks, such as MySpace and Facebook, came along in the mid-2000s. They consolidated previous communities scattered across the web. It became exponentially easier to find and connect with the people we wanted to, and now we're connected to more people than ever.

Today, while Gen Z rarely spends time on Facebook and MySpace is obsolete, social media platforms such as Instagram, Snapchat, and TikTok are where many young people get their first taste of digital connection. When done intentionally, such as Girl Genius' Instagram takeovers, social media is a powerful tool to gather people together and spark community.

Crowdsourcing

Along with the rise of social media networks came crowdsourcing content and empowering community members as creators. It's easier than ever for everyday users to contribute information instead of just consuming it.

Wikipedia is one of the first examples of crowdsourced knowledge at scale. Initially, Wikipedia started with peer-reviewed articles from experts only, which was highly inefficient and produced minimal content. To address that problem, they decided to ask for articles from community members who were historically content consumers. Surprisingly, the crowdsourced articles were comprehensive and well-written.

In fact, a study published in the journal *Nature* reveals Wikipedia is about as accurate as Britannica; whereas the average Britannica article has 2.92 errors, Wikipedia has 3.86. Wikipedia gets a bad rap from my teachers, but the difference in error rate per article between Wikipedia and the "trusted standard" of information is less than one!

Wikipedia revealed crowdsourcing is an effective method to organize and distill knowledge. Its community of contributors, called Wikimedians, ensures the quality of information brought forth by each individual member and self-corrects where necessary. As Wikimedians get to know each other, connect on deeper values (like the belief knowledge should be free), and build trust, they are more likely to act in ways that strengthen the community they have come to love.

Whether it be a crowdsourced Google Doc of college scholarships or local volunteer opportunities, Gen Zers have similarly harnessed the collective knowledge of communities to do what individuals are not able to accomplish alone. Along the way, being noticed and appreciated (and the responsibility that comes with it) encourages members to contribute as their best selves.

Curation

As crowdsourcing led to the proliferation of information, community building increasingly required content curation: the ability to scour the internet for specific resources and ideas that are valuable to your community. Offering high-quality content for a niche subject drives interest in the community, and context-specific, trustworthy information often serves as a foundation for collaboration.

Many thriving youth-centered digital communities today are built on curation—the idea that there is too much that exists out there on the internet, and busy Gen Zers need you to editorialize. Curating information allows communities to add value to a member's experience and help folks "get on the same page."

Winter BreeAnne is a young changemaker who works at the intersection of social justice, politics, and culture. Her advocacy work began when she founded the Instagram page Black is Lit after noticing a void in Black representation on the platform. She was tired of seeing the injustices around her and wanted to create a space to tell positive everyday stories of Black folks in her community.

The Instagram page (@blkislit) spotlights the work of Black creators/ activists/changemakers, shouts out Black-owned businesses, and amplifies the message of Black Lives Matter. Positive stories of Black people are not represented in the media enough, especially stories of Black people catalyzing social change and fighting for justice.

By curating stories through Black is Lit, Winter ensures other young changemakers don't need to dig for spirit-nourishing stories. They can come to the Instagram page and feel validated and empowered. Here, young Black changemakers can identify role models and see themselves reflected in social movements. Curation is powerful because it ensures viewers resonate with the content and will apply it in some way. Only the most relevant and useful stories are shared—stories that teach, inspire, educate, or create space for certain experiences.

Black is Lit's Instagram page has a simple bio: "Community. Everyday." Curation is key to how they nurture a sense of pride and power, and increase people's ability to take action together.

Online Organizing

Stories not only allow us to create shared narratives that build community, they also play a powerful role in illuminating injustice and catalyzing change. Through the practice of collecting stories that emerge from a group, digital communities have facilitated bottom-up, grassroots organizing driven by people's lived experiences. More and more young people are using social media to spark movements demanding action for issues surrounding racial justice, climate action, and gender equality.

March For Our Lives (MFOL) took off on social media, especially on Twitter, where Parkland students were able to own their narrative and mobilize supporters around the US. *The New York Times* writes, "With their consistent tweeting of stories, memes, jokes and video clips, the students have managed to keep the tragedy their school experienced—and their plan to stop such shootings from happening elsewhere—in the news for weeks, long after past mass shootings have faded from the headlines."

While people didn't magically form tight-knit communities overnight, MFOL's Twitter strategy sparked important conversations and attracted new advocates. Through their organization's social media posts, people learned something new, empathized with a different perspective, and experienced sadness, fear, and anger alongside millions of others. MFOL found a group of people who *cared.*

With thoughtful nudging (following up with individuals, sharing resources at strategic times, moving people into Slack channels and group chats), this care was molded into tangible forms of support. These online communities went on to power the coordination of hundreds of sister marches, voter registration drives, and donations from celebrities like George Clooney, Taylor Swift, and Oprah.

In an interview with NBC News, MFOL co-founder Lauren Hogg says, "So much of our success is in our community, in being together, in being able to see and support each other… This year [2020] has really stretched this idea of organizing and made us find a community over social media, over phone calls." Digital-first community building is a critical component of sustaining and growing grassroots movements.

Without digital communities, MFOL would not be possible. Decentralized movements require us to be able to easily discover, learn from, and build trust with folks who care about similar issues (with whom we might not be in the same physical location), so we can work toward shared goals.

* * *

It's important to note the four functions above are not separate and don't evolve in a linear fashion. Digital communities didn't "develop" from social networks to digital organizing. They exist side-by-side, often happening simultaneously and building off each other. For example, Girl Genius couldn't curate the best opportunities for women in STEAM if they didn't crowdsource from community members. And MFOL's online organizing definitely couldn't have happened without social networks like Twitter.

Digital communities have come a long way from the sparsely populated internet bulletin boards of the 1970s. They now influence everything from who we connect with and where we spend our time, to how we circulate information and make sense of the world.

Data from the Institute of Business Management reveals more than 74 percent of Gen Z says they spend their free time online. As the number of community parks, pools, libraries, coffee shops, and other physical public infrastructure decline, the internet offers greater accessibility and diversity of activities. Online, we can discover communities of fanfiction writers, BTS fans, mental health advocates, and others who might not exist in our neighborhoods. As Gen Zers flock to digital spaces, a pivotal question remains: Are digital communities as effective as in-person communities in supporting the development of young people?

Can digital communities ever match the value of in-person communities?

For many, the answer is no. There simply seem to be too many things, such as body language and emotion, that cannot be replicated online. Pizza parties, real hugs, and cheering for someone as they step into a room are small actions that build community, but which cannot be done through a screen.

That said, while digital communities may not "match the value" of in-person ones, they introduce new tools and ways of bringing people together across geographical, cultural, and ideological boundaries. What is "valuable" varies with criteria, such as physical intimacy or geographical diversity. It's unfair to compare in-person and digital-first. They each have their own strengths and capabilities that need to be evaluated in different ways. Instead of seeing them as direct replacements for each other, we need to start seeing them as complementary modes of community to help people find meaning and connection in their lives.

The complementary value of digital-first communities is clear. A recent study by Tapatalk revealed 64 percent of Gen

Zers and millennials feel more understood by specialized online communities than by family and real-world friends.

As a Gen Zer myself, I can second that statistic. Some of my closest friends today are from online communities like Civics Unplugged. And get this—I have never met a single one of them in person! Digital communities have given me incredible agency over whom I invite into my life, and I'm able to find folks with shared values, goals, and interests.

While digital communities haven't been perfect, from folks excluded because of limited internet access to toxic unmoderated Reddit threads, they have also been powerful tools for social and civic good. In an article from the Pew Research Center, futurist and author Byron Reese notes, "Anyone who has posted a question in a forum and received an answer from a stranger knows firsthand they bring us together. Wikipedia taught us strangers will work together for a common good. The open-source movement and Creative Commons showed people will labor for free to benefit strangers." Digital spaces have incredible potential to bring out the best in us, and help strangers coordinate and collaborate to tackle big problems.

Simply put, digital communities aren't second to physical ones. And community builders are constantly experimenting with new structures and processes from which even better ways of gathering online will emerge.

* * *

A final trend I'd like to touch on is the movement away from public-facing social platforms into private digital spaces. Fewer young people are broadcasting themselves into open spaces like Instagram, but rather practicing authenticity in smaller, more intimate platforms like Discord channels, WhatsApp group chats, and Minecraft servers.

Yancey Strickler, co-founder of Kickstarter and author of *This Could Be Our Future*, has similarly written about the struggle to be himself online. He describes his retreat away from public platforms like Twitter and Facebook, where it felt "too risky to be my real self... the downsides of saying something wrong or getting unwanted attention no longer felt worth it."

Strickler likens the internet to a dark forest, an idea introduced in the Chinese science fiction series *The Three Body Problem* by Liu Cixi. Here's how Strickler explains it in his blog article:

Imagine a dark forest at night. It's deathly quiet. Nothing moves. Nothing stirs. This could lead one to assume that the forest is devoid of life. But of course, it's not. The dark forest is full of life. It's quiet because night is when the predators come out. To survive, the animals stay silent.

Is our universe an empty forest or a dark one? If it's a dark forest, then only Earth is foolish enough to ping the heavens and announce its presence. The rest of the universe already knows the real reason why the forest stays dark. It's only a matter of time before the Earth learns as well.

This is also what the internet is becoming: a dark forest.

In response to the ads, the tracking, the trolling, the hype, and other predatory behaviors, we're retreating to our dark forests of the internet, and away from the mainstream.

The solution to the dark forest? Digital campfires.

There's a movement of young people into smaller, more intimate online destinations, which LA-based digital strategist Sara Wilson describes as *digital campfires*. "If social media can feel like a crowded airport terminal where everyone is allowed, but no one feels particularly excited to be there, digital campfires offer a more intimate oasis where smaller groups of people are excited to gather," Wilson wrote in the *Harvard Business Review*. Gen Zers are tired of feeling anonymous and want niche spaces filled where they are understood.

A report from RadiumOne estimates 69 percent of social sharing now happens on dark social channels, shielded from public view. Discord channels, Minecraft servers, and private newsletters lend themselves to smaller, personalized, and self-selecting communities. After all, Instagram group chats have a limit of thirty-two people, creating a natural cut-off point. In digital campfires, it's a lot easier to be our real selves and follow our curiosity without worrying about being judged. Especially when paired with guardrails such as barriers to entry, clear rules, and effective moderation, smaller digital spaces allow people to simply be.

Movements like March For Our Lives and the climate advocacy organization Zero Hour are discovering ways of online organizing that involve intentional community building through intimate video calls, not relying solely on social media blasts. Change happens at the speed of trust—yet many of us don't have access to enough digital spaces where we can be authentic, vulnerable, and build trust with each other. How do you build a movement with people if you don't even know them (beyond their 140-character opinion)?

The convergence of these trends is embodied by the rise of digital campfire-like communities outside of traditional social networks, such as Fortnite, Roblox, and Twitch. For Gen Z, gaming is more than just an entertainment; it's how we connect with friends. Video games such as Fortnite provide a common gathering ground and allow people to embark on shared journeys in the virtual world that help them bond. While Fortnite was originally intended to be a video game, it has evolved into a corner of the internet where people can get together, do something cool, and find their inner circle of friends.

* * *

It's clear digital communities aren't static. Traditional social networks have created increased optionality and access for folks who would otherwise never have been in the same space together. They have powered everything from MFOL to the spirit-nourishing stories from Black is Lit.

That said, broadcasting our authentic selves in public is scary. In the search for intimate connections, we are discovering new ways to connect through games, audio, and unconventional digital campfires. To be clear, the big social networks, crowdsourcing, and curation aren't going away; they are critical for movement building. But similar to how digital-first communities complement real-life interactions, smaller digital campfires are important complements to online public squares.

You might meet someone at a busy neighborhood park (a public space) and invite them over to tea at your home the next day (a smaller, more private one). Digital campfires are where trusted relationships and power are created.

1.3

WHY NOW: BENEFITS AND TRENDS

———

"We are caught in an inescapable network of mutuality, tied in a single garment of destiny. Whatever affects one directly, affects all indirectly."

—MARTIN LUTHER KING

I still remember my first time using Zoom.

In April 2017, I'd just been elected as a state officer for Washington Future Business Leaders of America (FBLA), a career and technical student organization preparing the next generation of community-minded business leaders. Like all the other newly elected officers, I pored over the State Officer Handbook, a thick binder of what-to-expect documents for the year. Because the fourteen state officers were located all across the state, we'd participate in monthly meetings on *Zoom*, the handbook said, in addition to our quarterly in-person meetings.

At that time, I didn't really think much of Zoom. The highlights of FBLA were the in-person conferences. If I was being honest, I didn't care much for our Zoom meetings, which were dull and somehow seemed to drag on forever. These meetings were always packed with agenda items. Often, we didn't even get a chance to ask how each other were doing before diving into attendance and committee updates. At any given moment, officers were yawning, had cameras off, or very clearly multitasking... people were on the call, but not really *present*.

Never could I imagine only a few years later, we'd spend the entire FBLA year on Zoom and host our state conference online.

It's crazy to think there was a time when Zoom was just a video-conferencing app start-ups and overachieving FBLA students used. Today, it's not just FBLA that has gone online during the pandemic. School, prom, book clubs, extracurriculars, even study abroad programs have as well. There is no doubt Zoom consumed my senior year of high school. I spent over ten hours a week alone in communities like Civics Unplugged, whether through Zoom calls or simply messaging people on Slack.

Maybe you've experienced something similar. What online communities have emerged or played an increasingly significant role in *your* life this past year? It seems like our lives exist in digital campfires these days. The question is, why?

The obvious reason is the pandemic. COVID-19 has been a forcing function for us to transition our lives online in order to protect ourselves and those around us. In fact, the pandemic was a catalyst behind my curiosity for digital-first community building.

In March 2020, my high school closed due to COVID. At first, like many of my classmates, I was ecstatic by the prospect of an extended Spring break. When three days turned into six weeks, which turned into the rest of the year online, I quickly went from happy to overwhelmed.

At that time, I was serving as the State President for Washington FBLA. Our State Business Leadership Conference (SBLC), the pinnacle of the FBLA experience for more than 2,000 members and advisers, was supposed to take place April 8-11, 2020. The state officer team spent months planning the conference, students spent the whole year preparing for competitions, and awards, conference materials, and plane tickets were already purchased. However, everything we knew was taken away in the blink of an eye.

There was simply no way for us to host the conference given the health and safety regulations in place.

Without the finality of an in-person SBLC and the anticipation of "going out with a bang," I could feel the state officer team drifting apart. At the same time, I was feeling a lot of pressure from the board of directors to help the officer team and our members to adapt to a new reality.

Zoom meetings, previously anathema, became a go-to for our team. They allowed us to preserve the structural experiences within our mini-FBLA officer team community, including monthly team meetings and personal development calls. To connect with our membership, we leveraged weekly adviser email blasts, Instagram stories, and new Zoom "coffee chats" with state officers.

Moving online presented the best solution for us all to stay connected, push forward, and accomplish everything we wanted to do.

And it isn't just FBLA. In clubs, teams, workspaces, and communities around the world, people were grasping for connection and the sense of purpose they had in person. COVID-19 accelerated our movement toward remote work and learning. Practically overnight, everything from the ping pong club to National Honor Society to Earth Day events pivoted online in order to keep folks engaged.

Zoom meetings and other forms of online connection are no longer a "nice-to-have" supplement to in-person communities. They are key tools to help people adapt to an increasingly virtual world.

* * *

While COVID-19 sparked a new wave of people searching for community online, it's important to note many people were moving toward online communities even before the pandemic. According to Our World in Data, an average of 640,000 people/day went online for the first time between 2010 and 2016. This is what has allowed Massive Open Online Courses, #FridaysForFuture, Fortnite communities, and other online spaces to take off.

Furthermore, a few societal trends have encouraged people to build digital-first communities to substitute or enhance in-person ones: rising loneliness and disconnection (in part due to the decline of physical public spaces), increasing emphasis on inclusion, and the emergence of bottom-up, grassroots movements.

Online communities are uniquely positioned to take advantage of these trends and provide solutions people are looking for.

Declining Physical Spaces and Rising Loneliness

Loneliness has been a growing problem for decades, largely due to the decline of physical public spaces and the communities that form in them. Physical social infrastructure—the public spaces where people congregate and bond with each other—are rapidly disappearing. According to a 2018 Gallup poll, church membership in the US has declined by more than 20 percent since 1999, most of the decline attributable to the rise of people with no religious affiliation. Mark Chaves, a sociology professor at Duke University, estimates in *The New York Times* that 3,500 churches close their doors each year. And it's not just churches. The Institute of Museum and Library Services reports per person library visits and reference transactions declined over the ten-year period from 2008 to 2017, by 17.5 percent and 24.9 percent, respectively. According to Mick Nelson, senior director of aquatic facilities development at USA Swimming, over 1,800 community pools have closed since 2009.

These statistics are jarring, because churches, libraries, community pools, and other public spaces are critical to cultivating relationships among friends and neighbors. In his book *Palaces for the People*, American sociologist Eric Klinenberg writes, "People forge ties in places that have healthy social infrastructures—not necessarily because they set out to build community, but because when people engage in sustained, recurrent interaction, particularly while doing things they enjoy, relationships—even across ethnic or political lines—[community] inevitably grows."

In his seminal work *Bowling Alone: America's Declining Social Capital*, researcher Robert Putnam describes how over the past few decades, physical communities such as youth service clubs and bowling leagues have experienced steep declines in membership. The amount of time we spend in public spaces, much less being vulnerable in them, have declined. If the nearest bowling league was thirty miles away, would you make the drive? Probably not.

People are unconsciously spending less time building communities in physical spaces, because an increasing number of those spaces no longer exist! Instead, we retreat to isolated spaces we *do* have access to, like automobiles and personal headphones. Not surprisingly, removing opportunities to see each other decreases chances for connection.

Fewer connections mean eroding communities, which mean even fewer opportunities to get to know people. This forms a negative feedback loop that results in loneliness. In fact, a 2018 survey by the health company Cigna shows nearly half of Americans report sometimes or always feeling alone or left out.

Loneliness is a subjective feeling where the connections we need are greater than the connections we have. This gap diminishes feelings of belonging that are critical to community. It causes people to withdraw from the collective and retreat into themselves. We forget there are people who love and want to help us, if we only ask for their support. We forget what it feels like to get together, pool together our resources, and make collective decisions.

For many young people, loneliness leads to powerlessness. Suddenly, they no longer have the ability to care for themselves or those around them.

To combat this rise in isolation and lack of meaningful relationships, young people must create new ways to congregate. Physical public infrastructure has become fragmented, less inclusive, or even nonexistent. Digital communities are a promising supplement, if not an alternative, for people to find connection and belonging.

One of the most powerful examples of digital communities meeting the need for human connection is captured in *Palaces for the People*, where Klinenberg talks about the Brooklyn Library's "Library Lanes"—virtual Xbox-based bowling leagues that meet weekly inside the basements and community centers of libraries. Virtual bowling pits local seniors in friendly competition with teams from other library branches. It's not about who wins, but rather the camaraderie that forms within and across teams, created by seniors cheering each other on, proudly sporting the same bowling jerseys, and having fun together. In this way, connecting to a screen becomes a legitimate method for building community.

What makes Library Lanes powerful is it alludes to Robert Putnam's *Bowling Alone* article, in which he makes the case that technology is the primary evil that caused people to leave clubs and encouraged people to spend leisure time on their own. "Social media allows people to feel like they are in a kind of community, but they don't actually have deep relationships in them," Putnam argues.

But what happened in Brooklyn and what young people are realizing around the world is that when used thoughtfully, technology is a powerful tool to create shared experiences. Online spaces add to our social infrastructure, not detract from them.

Scaling Impact and Radical Inclusion

First and foremost, digital-first communities done correctly can transcend the geographical, cultural, and ideological barriers that often exist in the real world. For example, as someone who lives in Vancouver, WA, it's pretty hard for me to spontaneously hang out with friends in India. And because I live fifteen minutes away from Portland, OR, a city famous for its progressive politics, it requires conscious effort to search for independent or conservative perspectives. Historically inconvenient experiences became exponentially easier online. I'm now able to access diverse perspectives without the opportunity cost of time and travel. Even more exciting, this enables impact-oriented youth organizations to leverage digital communities for unprecedented scale and impact.

Peace First is a nonprofit organization supporting a youth-led movement to build a more just and peaceful world. They empower innovators ages thirteen to twenty-five with one-to-one mentorship, a caring community of peers, up to $25,000 of project funding, and storytelling initiatives that celebrate their impact. All of this takes place on the Peace First platform—the world's largest digital marketplace for youth-led social change initiatives.

Digital tools and digital communities power almost everything Peace First does. Recruiting, coaching, and distributing grants to young people in over 135 countries is only possible through an innovative combination of email newsletters, Zoom calls, WhatsApp group chats, and the Peace First digital platform. It seems like Peace First has it down, but what's surprising is they didn't always operate this way.

Peace First originally started as a student-run program at Harvard University, where it developed young peacemakers through in-person, school-based programming. This work produced powerful results, such as a 60 percent decrease in disruptive incidents at schools and 81 percent of students reporting they could walk away from a fight.

However, working in physical schools didn't maximize Peace First's full potential. At the time when staff members concentrated efforts in school systems, Peace First was a multimillion-dollar organization delivering programs to a small slice of schools and students. Between site coordinators, teacher trainers, and parent engagement liaisons, Peace First was expending too many resources on just one school. They experienced the limitations of in-person organizing and community building. The model simply did not support their mission at scale.

Peace First's leadership asked themselves: How might we effectively train and connect young peacemakers from around the world? They realized that to scale sustainably, they would need to build a digital community. Since pivoting online, Peace First has been able to accomplish so much more than they were before. Instead of serving students at a handful of schools in the US, they now reach thousands of students around the world.

And building digital community doesn't mean Peace First completely removed in-person programming. The team still hosts annual summits and various conference-style events. The digital community aspect simply allows the organization to deepen connections from in-person events, keep their community alive when physically apart, and decrease the barrier of access.

Building Movements to Tackle Complex Problems

Our world is facing a number of critical issues increasing in complexity and size every day. These issues, from the climate crisis to rising inequality to rapidly deteriorating democratic systems, will not be solved by any one individual or community. The speed at which these problems are evolving, powered by rapid technological progress, demands greater coordination to come up with solutions.

The intersectional nature of these challenges requires people from all generations, geographies, cultures, ideologies, and identities to work together. While immense scale and inclusion is hard to achieve in-person, it becomes more feasible online.

For example, the climate strike movement took off with #FridaysForFuture, which started when fifteen-year-old Greta Thunberg and other young activists refused to go to school for three weeks. Instead, they sat in front of the Swedish parliament to protest lack of action on the climate crisis. Greta posted her actions on Instagram and Twitter, and it soon went viral. Young people drew inspiration from what their peers were doing in Sweden and adapted it to fit their local context. Instead of Greta telling her friends one-by-one to join the movement, thousands of students around the world learned about the movement through the hashtag. Instead of taking action alone, people teamed up across geographical boundaries to strike together.

Needless to say, digital organizing has been a huge part of the climate activism strategy.

During the onset of the COVID-19 pandemic, it became clear digital-first community building is the surest way to maintain momentum, hold people in power accountable, and ensure climate issues are at the forefront of the presidential election agenda.

In celebration of the fiftieth anniversary of Earth Day on April 22, 2020, youth climate activists had been planning what was to be the largest climate strike in history. When it became clear it needed to be canceled due to social distancing restrictions, organizers quickly pivoted online. Leaders from the US Climate Strike and Stop the Money Pipeline Coalition created Earth Day Live, a seventy-two-hour livestream where millions of people would join activists, celebrities, and musicians in an epic moment of community and hope for the future.

Earth Day featured celebrity cameos and high-profile speakers, from politicians like Stacey Abrams and Rep. Alexandria Ocasio-Cortez, to performers such as Ziggy Marley and Jason Mraz. The three-day agenda was bursting with morning yoga sessions, meditation moments, musical performances, DJ'd sets for evening dance parties, even sessions for cooking, gardening, and a collective clap for frontline workers. Through digital community building, Earth Day Live drew in millions of people, amplified the voices of indigenous leaders and youth climate activists, educated attendees on divestment and climate financing, and made climate issues a priority for upcoming voters.

While organizers were unable to do the strike they had originally planned, this new online event was even more successful than they could have imagined. Dillon Bernard from the Future Coalition, one of the key organizers of Earth Day Live, summarizes it well. "When we're able to go back into the streets, I think our movement will be stronger," he told *The Verge*. "People who have never been to an in-person strike before might tune into a livestream. Celebrities who otherwise wouldn't have been able to join the Earth Day program might be inspired and decide to stay involved."

Other youth-centered climate organizations, such as the Sunrise Movement, built on the momentum of digital-first communities. Instead of continuing voter registration drives on college campuses after Earth Day, they launched Sunrise School, which connects young people passionate about climate change, coronavirus, police violence, and the state of the world. Through an online community and a cohort-based learning experience, Sunrise School has helped more than 10,000 students build the knowledge and skills they need to confront these crises.

Sunrisers are also finding other ways to strengthen the climate movement online. One of their key actions is phone banking, person-to-person conversations that build support for Sunrise-endorsed politicians. While the act of making phone calls to strangers doesn't seem very inspiring (especially when you receive negative responses, like people hanging up on you or not picking up at all), Sunrise has discovered ways to make it an empowering, connection-centered experience.

First, in large Zoom calls, Sunrise facilitators explain how to phone bank. Callers have a chance to meet each other, then break off to make calls on their own. Most participants keep their cameras on and simply mute themselves, so they can still see each other's faces and reactions. In the Zoom chat, participants share successes and frustrations in real time. Messages like "WOO! Fifty-five people in here!" and "We're building PEOPLE POWER" are common, spreading positive energy like wildfire.

In fact, phone-banking is an antidote to loneliness for many Sunrise callers. "It's easy to feel isolated, but we're fed up with feeling sick and scared," says Yara, a Sunrise caller. "I've actually made many new friends [through Sunrise] since quarantine. On election nights, we get together on Google hangouts so we can be anxious together and watch videos." By providing a digital community and enabling young people to take action together, Sunrise helps them gain agency in a time where many feel anxious and powerless. And it's not just Sunrise and climate justice groups—this pattern of harnessing community power to drive change has been seen through everything from Bernie Sanders memes (Bernie wouldn't have been as popular among Gen Z in the 2020 election had he not been such a meme-able candidate) to #blacklivesmatter (now one of the most widely recognized and supported movements globally).

Think of a change needed in the world today. It can be about any topic, from geopolitical conflicts to effective altruism to access to youth entrepreneurship education. I'd wager regardless of the topic you're thinking of, digital-first communities have shaped that issue in some way and mobilized people to act.

Digital-first communities are the infrastructure behind today's most effective global movements. They have the potential to power so many more.

* * *

It's clear digital communities are needed more than ever in a world of rising loneliness, complex problems, and the need for coordinated action towards solutions. Imagine if youth climate activists didn't organize Earth Day Live and other digital events. What would've happened to the climate movement's momentum and resulting impact?

Now, think about all the other movements and spaces where thriving digital communities don't yet exist. Think about the things you are passionate about, whether that's increasing female representation in STEAM, supporting first-generation, low-income college students, country music, running, or something else entirely. Think about the complex, systemic issues in the world you would like to learn about and solve. Think about all the groups you belong to, and whether they're currently increasing your ability to tackle those issues.

My hypothesis is that individualism runs rampant because we lack spaces where we can work towards something together, in a spirit of collaboration instead of competition. Too often, we live in a zero-sum game with a finite set of resources and opportunities. Competing with others is the only way to get what we need. But given the chance to be part of flourishing communities and take action with others, I believe most of us are eager to contribute to the common good.

Digital communities have incredible potential to supercharge personal and systems change. The world needs community builders, now more than ever. Even if you're new to online communities or have never been part of one, don't automatically exclude yourself. One of the most powerful ways to learn how to build online communities is to contribute to existing ones. That, you can start doing today.

2.1

TWO PROVOCATIONS, A METAPHOR, AND THE CANVAS

———

"Gardening is not just a set of tasks. It's not restricted to backyards, courtyards, balconies. It can, and should, happen anywhere, everywhere. Gardening is simply a framework for engagement with our world, grounded in care and action. To garden is to care deeply, inclusively, and audaciously for the world outside our homes and our heads. It's a way of being that is intimately interwoven with the real truths of existence—not the things we're told to value (money, status, ownership), but the things that actually matter (sustenance, perspective, beauty, connection, growth)."

—GEORGINA REID

So, where do we start with community building?

It's hard to understand the importance of digital-first communities, much less cultivate flourishing ones, if you've never experienced it before. It's like telling someone to draw a flower they've never seen or do a math problem they never learned. To those of you who have stumbled upon digital-first communities before, consider yourselves lucky. If you haven't, know you're not alone.

When we aren't able to experience community firsthand, *imagining* is an ideal alternative.

This book is filled with provocations. I'm not here to "sell" you on the right way to build digital-first community. People have been doing this for decades, using all sorts of methodologies that evolve at an increasingly rapid pace. Instead, I hope it helps you imagine what better futures might look like for your online groups. I hope you gain the confidence to set audacious goals for your community and the frameworks and processes you need to bring them into reality.

Ultimately, I hope this book prompts you to examine why your community looks the way it looks. What are the structures, processes, and cultures that exist in your community? How do members show up and interact with each other?

Become aware of mental models—the set of unconscious, default assumptions—you bring into community building. Understanding the lens through which you view the world creates space for new lenses that introduce new possibilities. If you believe people are fundamentally separate individuals who need to compete with each other over scarce resources, it's hard to imagine mutual aid or even spending time to care for others' emotional needs. When your stories, beliefs, and dreams change, your community's structures and practices will follow.

Becoming aware is why provocations are important. Provocations—phrases, questions, images, and other artifacts that spark thought, wonder, and curiosity—can be controversial but true in possibly many ways. They are open to interpretation. The objective of provocations is simple: to provoke a new train of thought, bring competing perspectives to the surface, or create space for paradox. Provocations encourage us to explore the full range of opportunities available to our communities. To begin, here are two key provocations.

Decentralize Power

Community building is about sharing power. Without power, members simply aren't able to translate their energy and imagination into making the community better.

Furthermore, communities create space for not only emotional support, but also other forms of mutual aid, whether that's sharing money, information, or social networks. When people support each other and make decisions together, they gain agency over the future of their own lives and the world around them.

In community, young people are able to rely less on adult structures of power. For instance, take a peer tutoring initiative. Instead of waiting for a teacher to explain the answer, fellow community members can offer support and teach what they know. And it's not just young people—marginalized communities are also able to extract themselves from traditional, often oppressive structures of power. Immigrant communities who self-organize lending circles instead of waiting for traditional VC funding (which they disproportionately receive less of) become more self-sufficient and powerful on their own.

That said, communities don't always decentralize power. The default way of organizing our groups today is hierarchical. Just think of the typical student club leadership... it's almost a given there's a president, vice president, secretary, and treasurer. Isn't it unfortunate that power—both decision-making and influence—centralize at the very top? We preach that everyone is powerful but fail to create organizational structures that embody our beliefs. Instead, we have to count on the people at the top to *empower* us and be benevolent enough to share some of their power, which is usually impossible to do. People with power tend to hold on to it by rigging the game so *they* benefit.

How might we think ahead and design our communities so they allow people to practice power at the smallest scales?

Lead with Love

It can often seem like the sole purpose of clubs, communities, and youth-led initiatives is to accomplish things. Maybe you're focused on successfully pulling off a virtual fundraiser, helping club members qualify for the national competition, or fighting against one of the many injustices in the world. We're often stuck in this go-go-go space, a never-ending battle to do more.

While this urgency to take action can fuel us in the short run, it is not sustainable. Few are willing to return when an organization forgets to take care of people first.

Storyteller and anti-racism facilitator Verta Maloney often says, "All love, with appropriate doses of rage"—something that couldn't resonate with me more. What is radical is not always resistance or speaking truth to power (which is overemphasized in youth activism), but rather openness and compassion. In the long run, love is what sustains us. People come back to spaces where they feel acknowledged and appreciated, not just for their contributions, but for simply being themselves.

If you were in a space where you constantly had to prove yourself by working 200 times as hard, how long would you stay? Contrast that with a space where you're treated as a trusted community member and challenged with opportunities to stretch and grow. The famous poet Goethe once wrote, "If we treat people as if they were what they ought to be, we help them become what they are capable of being." That is what leading with love means: to treat community members in ways (through empathy, gratitude, authenticity) that help them realize their full potential.

How might we create safe space in our communities for people to become the truest expressions of themselves?

* * *

Beyond the two provocations, there's another concept that might spark your imagination. It is a metaphor and perhaps a provocation in itself: community as a garden.

One of the clearest ways the metaphor makes sense is through a community builder's role. Sometimes, new leaders believe building community between people is fostered by executing discrete actions, like adding more people or more events. To them, community is more of a machine than a garden. They believe just like how you put quarters in a gumball machine and get gumballs out, you can put people in a group chat and get amazing relationships out.

Unfortunately, it doesn't quite work like that.

Being a community "builder" is slightly misleading. Community isn't built out of thin air, nor is it a linear process with defined inputs and outputs. Community is something constantly emerging and evolving with the relationships between members. Relationships are formed by members choosing to lean in, not because you've pieced together people in some calculated way. A better verb to describe what you do might be to **tend**: care for or look after; give one's attention to, or to **steward**: to take care of something. As the community builder, your job isn't to force community to happen. Instead, you're here to create the right conditions for community to emerge and care for the space that is formed.

Community isn't just about introducing a bunch of people to each other; it's about growing the relationships between everyone lovingly like you'd grow a plant.

I built my first plant terrarium earlier this year and can attest calling myself a gardener draws out my kinder, more loving side. It gave me a new framework for thinking about the world: caring for myself and the needs of others with care and rapt attention. My plants require sunlight, water, and nutrients regularly. The plant tells me what it needs by looking droopy, and when I notice the crinkling leaves, it reminds me to check in with my own body. This is how we should treat the people in our communities—looking out for subtle signs of change and acting on them.

Instead of trying to build communities like we're building a company, what happens if we treat the process like tending gardens?

Just like plants need different things to thrive and contribute to the ecosystem, community members do too. Just like how plants lean on each other and form symbiotic relationships, we might notice how interconnected our communities are and become increasingly generous in giving and accepting support. Most importantly, just like how gardens grow and evolve, we might start to see community as a living organism that doesn't need someone to "lead" it, but rather to care for it—removing weeds, trimming leaves, covering the garden bench with a fresh layer of paint.

My friend Maryam talks about how tending gardens has taught her what it means to be a community steward. "Maybe your role in a community is simply to get it started and let it take on a life of its own. Maybe you're supposed to start out super involved and slowly fade out over time, pruning here and there when needed. And maybe you're a constant fixture, regularly adding new plants, moving things around, re-landscaping, and creating a blueprint for future communities." The metaphor of digital gardens helps us embrace the livingness of our communities and the ever-shifting roles we are called to take on.

Part 2 of the book (the section you're on now!) is grounded in the garden metaphor. How might we cultivate communities differently if we saw how they resemble living systems and treat them as such?

The following chapters follow the life cycle of a community steward. If you're new to cultivating communities, it would make the most sense to read them in order. Otherwise, identify where you are in the process and start there. For example, if you've already found your people and have them onboarded into a community Slack channel, it would make the most sense to start on Chapter 2.4: Creating Space.

Community is not linear, and stewardship does not imply ownership over the process. You might start reading a certain chapter and realize you need to go "back" or iterate through the chapters a couple of times. That is to be expected! After all, gardening is a messy process that, more often than not, resembles organized chaos. Plants are going to die and rot, support stakes do fall over, and vines inevitably get tangled together.

Embrace the process and use the book in whatever way best supports you. Feel free to read forward, backward, or simply choose the chapters that feel meaningful. Here are the chapters, along with short descriptions of what to expect.

Gather your supplies:

- **2.2: Find your people** // decide on the plants. Before we can build communities, we have to find people and a reason to bring them together. This chapter talks about crafting barriers to entry and delightful onboarding processes.
- **2.3: Technology** // choose a location. Since we're building digital-first communities, finding technology is the equivalent of finding a physical meeting venue and decorating it! Location can have a huge impact on how people show up.

Cultivate the garden:

- **2.4: Create space** // situate your plan. A community builder's role is creating space for community to emerge, a space where people can show up as their authentic selves and contribute their gifts to the collective. Rules and effective facilitation help this happen.
- **2.5: Facilitate transformation** // create experiences that level up your garden. After space has been created, what goes in it? What do people do together? Rituals and learning experiences are transformative events people buy into.

Find new stewards:

- **2.6: Capture your vibe** // document what makes your garden special. As you think about helping the community self-organize, how do aesthetics, culture, vibe, and stories shape its legacy and growth?
- **2.7: Empower new leaders** // discover new garden tenders. At some point, it's time for the community steward to pass on the torch, so new members can dedicate their time and energy to the community. How might we smoothen this transition?

* * *

Finally, before we dive into the nitty gritty details of digital-first community building, there's a tool that has been incredibly helpful for me to zoom out and look at the structural components of community: the Community Canvas.

For the longest time, I thought no rhyme or reason existed in community building. From the outside, every community looked and felt so different. I knew certain online communities took off and others didn't, but never asked why. I thought it was a hit or miss thing, and community builders were just lucky they hopped on the right trend and found fans obsessed with what their communities stood for.

It's really all just luck and good timing, right?

Either that, or community builders could do magic. It just seemed crazy that any one person could organize and coordinate digital communities of hundreds of people toward a single cause. How much brain space does that even take? All the logistics and planning and relationships and details?

I didn't know where to start with digital-first community building. And I never considered there could be a shared framework underlying the development of them all.

Imagine my surprise when I came across the Community Canvas.

The Community Canvas is a play on the Lean Canvas, a concept from the start-up world that helps founders communicate the basic structures of their business or social venture. Similarly, the Community Canvas helps community builders think about and communicate the basic structures of their community.

The Canvas is composed of three sections, each of which represents a key pillar of community. Here are the sections:

- **Identity** // belonging: who and what? Community builders and members belong to communities, but the community itself also belongs to people who have to put a part of themselves into co-creating it.
- **Experience** // trust: when, where, and why? Everything moves at the speed of trust—and trust within communities is built on the knowledge members have of each other. This knowledge is developed over time by constantly showing up and engaging in shared experiences.
- **Structure** // resilience: how, and if this, then what? There will undoubtedly be fights, disagreements, and unpredicted things that happen. How does the community respond and make decisions when things go south?

As you can imagine, rigorously examining these three sections, and the seventeen themes within them, is useful. The Canvas comes with an online guidebook, which includes further background, observations, and key questions for each theme, to help community builders apply these ideas.

Fabian, Nico, and Sascha, the trio behind the Canvas, also created the Minimum Viable Community (MVC): a one-page mini-canvas with nine of the most critical themes and its questions to help new community builders get their communities off the ground. The MVC is just enough for prospective members to gain a stronger understanding of the values and goals of your community.

The Community Canvas helped me realize a couple things.

First, it surprised me that start-up-y language appeared in the community space. I'd associated start-ups with rigorous processes and metrics, and communities with fluid, softer relationships. Realizing community building follows a methodological process made me take it seriously.

Second, the Canvas made me pause and say, "Wow, there's a formula to community building?" This was when it really clicked—I don't have to be an extrovert to build community. If I can follow this process and craft thoughtful answers to the questions, what's holding any of us back from creating a community that takes off?

Most importantly, I was able to use the Community Canvas to design the Youth Organizers Collective (YOC), a digital-first community that provides high school students the relationships, support, and knowledge they need to cultivate strong online clubs and organizations. I started the YOC as an experiment in March 2020, in response to COVID-19, schools going online, and feeling disconnected from previously in-person communities.

One of the first things I did for the YOC was write out my answers to all seventy-six questions in the guidebook and fill out a MVC canvas to share with others, from adult supporters to prospective community members.

Hands down, discovering the Community Canvas was the best thing that ever happened, and filling it out was the best decision I could've made.

If you're like me and naturally have a bias toward action, it might feel weird to ponder over the questions in the Canvas. You might bemoan the amount of time it takes to answer the questions thoroughly. Do it! As you dig into the questions, you'll see why. The Canvas prompts you to think about structures and processes behind communities you might've never considered otherwise.

It sounds simple, but I didn't realize I needed to have "success definitions" for my community (question four on the MVC). On second thought, it makes so much sense! If we don't define success, how can we figure out how to achieve it? Depending on what I was measuring success by (number or diversity of members, depth of connection), successful communities could look very different.

Parts of the upcoming chapters will reference and expand upon the ideas provided in the Community Canvas (https:// community-canvas.org/). Consider downloading the Canvas and Guidebook to follow along! These tools will help you think methodologically and *with intention* about community building, which makes you multiple times more effective.

* * *

The final thing I will say before we dive into the how-to section of the book is a vision for what a flourishing community looks like. What does flourishing—realizing one's full potential—look like on a community level? What types of online spaces are we trying to create?

Imagine a community where...

- **Relationships flourish**: People in the community trust and feel connected to each other. They show up. They feel a persistent sense of belonging. Members have discovered a sanctuary where they are accepted and loved for being themselves. People discover their inner circle of friends.
- **Everyone finds their you-shaped hole**: People feel like they've found a role in the community at the intersection of their values, strengths, passions, and long-term goals. It's what *they* are uniquely positioned to do. This role is meaningful and deserving of great dedication. It gives people ownership and responsibility for the community.
- **People practice real power**: People in the community have shared context, good communication, and a common vision for where they'd like to go. Power dynamics are consciously talked about and addressed. Everyone has access to information, relationships, capital, and other resources they need to lead.
- **Community grows and evolves on its own**: The community has documented and battle-tested processes that enable it to do what it was created to do. It self-corrects and evolves without a centralized authority. Many generations of stewards have listened and responded to the community's evolutionary purpose.

This flourishing community is possible, and you can help cultivate it.

2.2

FIND YOUR PEOPLE

---

*"Never join a camping party that has among its members
a single peevish, irritable, or selfish person, or a 'shirk.'
Although the company of such a boy may be only slightly
annoying at school or upon the playground, in camp the
companionship of a fellow of this description becomes
unbearable... The whole party should be composed
of fellows who are willing to take things as they come
and make the best of everything. With such compan-
ions there is no such thing as "bad luck"; rain or shine
everything is always jolly, and when you return from the
woods, strengthened in mind and body, you will always
remember with pleasure your camping experience."*

—D. C. BEARD

There is no doubt people are the most critical components
of a community.

Just like how a garden doesn't exist without plants, a community doesn't exist without people. Community members

are the ones who consistently show up with good vibes and take initiative to create transformative experiences that make the community healing, enlightening, and exciting.

Because people are so important, it is tempting to tie the success of our communities to simple metrics, like the number of people we have. For example, a 3,000-member Facebook group *sounds* a lot more impressive than a fifty-member one. There are many external incentives, from college applications to grants, that measure "impact." These vanity metrics make it tempting to just let anyone join the community in order to optimize for the most impressive size.

Playing the numbers game is one of the biggest mistakes new community builders make. It's critical to not be corrupted by these extrinsic motivators and remember "finding your people" takes time and intention.

YOU decide how big your community is, recognizing the tradeoff between size of the group and intimacy between members. There is no right or wrong size; for example, I might be able to be more vulnerable in a seven-person Zoom meeting than a 2,000-listener podcast. That said, a larger podcast community might be more effective in sharing a message with the world.

What should not be sacrificed with size is the rigorous process through which you select community members.

Think about it this way: It's not the size of a garden that determines whether it's healthy. Instead, it's which plants are there and how they are placed. Choosing the right plants is one of the most basic things you can do to help a garden thrive. For example, choose plants that like full sun for sunny locations and plants that like shade for shady locations. Give plants the right type of soil and the right amount of space they need. Ideally, your garden isn't a monoculture, and a variety of colors and textures complement each other. If you want a larger garden, you'll have to monitor it at a larger scale. While it might require more effort and time, it's not impossible with the right number of gardeners. What's not acceptable regardless of garden size is complacency. Complacency results in ugly, underdeveloped, or even dead plants, which doesn't bode well for your garden. For example, imagine if you decided that because you had a hundred plants, too many to water every day, you'd water none of them at all... not a good idea.

As UX designer Annika Izora explains in a recent interview with New_ Public, "It's not exactly the smallness or the size of the group that lends itself to the flourishing. The flourishing is rooted in 'What is the intention of this group of people in this space?'" Both small groups and large groups can be community-like if you choose the right people. You'll need outreach, selection, and onboarding processes that help you find folks whose strengths, passions, values, and long-term goals complement each other. Together, this group of people will flourish and give life to your community.

Ultimately, community building is a curation game—how do you find the right people and invite them to co-create the community you've imagined?

In this chapter, we explore the process of finding your people: how to craft ideal member personas, execute outreach and selection, and create welcoming onboarding processes that engage members. These steps might seem complex, but the time spent on finding people is essential to the flourishing of your community.

* * *

Pre-outreach Process

That's right, there's a pre-outreach process. If you're already working on text messages to invite your friends to join your budding community, hold your horses. Before you can invite people, you have to figure out what type of people you want to invite!

This is a great time to pull out the Community Canvas and reflect on the questions found in the Identity section, specifically around the purpose, identity, and values themes. Questions like "Who is the community for?" and "What are the traits members share?" are good places to start when crafting your ideal community member persona.

You might notice questions in the Canvas direct you to think about two big things: who the community members are (identity) and why they are gathering (purpose).

Get Together: How to Build a Community with Your People is a book written by Bailey Richardson, Kai Elmer Sotto, and Kevin Huynh, the founders of People & Co.—a company that coaches organizations like Nike, Substack, and the Surfrider Foundation to build communities with increased confidence. In the book, they emphasize the importance of starting with two questions:

- **Who do I want to get together?** In order for a community to take off, you'll need passionate members who are able and willing to invest time and energy to help set it up. This initial group will shape early rules and experiences, which then shape your community's culture and vibe—so it's critical they embody community values.
- **Why are we coming together?** Thriving communities demand a shared purpose. A shared purpose gives people

a reason to come together over and over again and helps ground the community in members' passions and interests. One measure of a flourishing community is whether people feel like they've found a "you-shaped hole"—a role in the community that is meaningful to them and deserving of great dedication.

These two questions don't need to be answered in order. You'll find your community's "reason for existing" naturally answers one of the questions, and you'll focus on the other.

For example, if you start with why (mission-driven communities, such as those advocating for the removal of standardized tests or increased access to healthy foods), you'll think about the who. Consider questions like: Who is affected by this issue? Who cares about this issue? How might you enlist people you have something in common with to care about the issue as well?

Other communities start with who (identity-based communities, such as a group of Taiwanese immigrants in Vancouver, WA, or migrant workers with young children). In these scenarios, think about why it's important for this specific group to meet again and again. Consider questions like: What do the people in this group need more of? What change do people desire? What is the problem this group is uniquely positioned to solve together?

Remember communities are always "for" someone. You are bringing a group of people together around a common interest, with the idea that each member contributes something special, receives something meaningful, and the members collectively create something useful. People who care about similar issues or have a useful skill are who your community is "for." Others won't be a good fit. It may be helpful to develop key personas to help you clarify the profile of an ideal community member and their demographics, behaviors, and goals.

The process for creating a persona is simple: If you already have a friend in mind who would be a perfect fit for the community, start with them. On a blank page, write down everything about them, their age, gender, interests, background, and personality. What characteristics make this specific friend a good person to invite? As you work, remember the ultimate goal is to remove personally identifiable details and create a persona that represents an entire segment of your community.

It's worth noting multiple people should understand the selection process and help you make decisions, so consider inviting existing community members to help select new ones. As you find your people, consult multiple perspectives and let these personas serve as a north star. If you're unsure whether someone is a good fit, check how aligned they are with the traits you identified in your ideal community member persona. Not everyone will match perfectly, and that's okay. Don't be too picky or else no one will be able to join! It's all about finding a balance.

* * *

Outreach and Selection Process

Now that you have your personas, the next step is to identify and reach out to prospective community members! This might be the first time you share your vision for the community with others. It's a nerve-wracking process. That said, finding your people is also an exciting opportunity to validate your idea. It allows you to test assumptions and see if this community is something people are looking for. You'll likely iterate the who and why of your community, and with practice, get better at describing what the community is and why it's so important.

Before we dive into specific strategies around outreach and selection, here are some broad concepts to keep in mind:

- **Do not try to appeal to everyone!** You've created personas for the ideal community member—let those personas guide you. Do not compromise the quality of community members for quantity.
- **Find ways to share your personas publicly.** When you are clear about who your community is for, people will notice and self-select into it if they feel like they would belong. It's a win-win for everyone!
- **Get comfortable with rejection; don't take it personally.** Putting your vision out there is one of the most personal things a community builder can do. We hope our community cuts through the noise (many communities exist, which is a good thing!). Sometimes it does, sometimes it doesn't. Don't be discouraged if it takes you some time to find your people or if you pivot your idea.

Reaching Out

So, what does it *actually* look like to find and ask people to join your community?

First, there's a simple decision you have to make: how do you define success for your community? Again, there's no right or wrong answer to this question. Are you thinking about the number of people? The diversity of people? The quality of conversations? Depending on your target community size and goals, you will implement different recruitment strategies.

It's worth reemphasizing that a large group does not equal flourishing, so don't feel pressured to write down a super big number. Communities are all about small experiments at scale, so it's totally fine (even encouraged) to test events with a smaller group before building a fully-fledged community. Smaller allows you to iterate rapidly and creates a strong foundation for your community to scale, if that's what you desire!

New community builders can also have a misconception that they need to reach a critical mass of members for their community to get off the ground. But because they never set a number for their critical mass, the outreach process drags on forever. People cycle in and out, as those who previously committed lose their interest with nothing happening. Community builders get caught up in elaborate social media ads and marketing funnels, and ultimately never move past the outreach-only phase.

Here's a secret: In every community, outreach is ongoing. There are certain points where you'll bring in new people, such as times when your community goes through a change in leadership or tackles new projects. The key is to not see outreach and other aspects of community building as linear, discrete steps. It will be messy and overlap. Don't feel like you have to be "done" with outreach before moving on with the next chapters… You never will be.

It's great to set a target for outreach and to shoot for it. That said, be flexible and realize goalposts can change. As members find value in your community, they will want to invite their friends. Organic growth in the middle of a community's life cycle is most sustainable. To achieve that, start providing value as soon as possible (we'll get into how to do so in the next couple of chapters).

In the meantime, use the strategies below to build a streamlined, time-bound plan for outreach!

Intimate Asks

For communities of all sizes, finding your first people can be as simple as creating a flyer on Canva and directly messaging it to twenty friends. This can take just thirty minutes—don't overcomplicate the process!

Personal asks are essential early on, because they allow you to...

- **Target the people you want.** You have full control over who you invite. Direct message the people who best fit the ideal community member personas you created earlier. These people are well positioned to help your community grow.
- **Leverage your personal brand.** No matter who you are, you have fans already, so start using it! You don't need to have a certain number of followers on social media. Think about family, friends, teachers, teammates, summer camp buddies... Everyone has a platform; it just comes in different forms. In the beginning of your community building journey, you're less likely to sell the community (since it's still being created and doesn't exist yet), and more likely to sell yourself as an individual. People might not buy into your vision yet, but still join the community because they believe in YOU! Getting people in the door is the first step to help them experience the magic of your community.

- **Make people feel special**. If community is all about helping people feel like they are seen and belong, the *process* of finding community members should embody these values. Every community member, whether the first or the hundredth, should feel warmly welcomed. Think about how special it feels to be remembered and invited to a birthday party and replicate that experience for your community.
- **Tap into scarcity and FOMO**. These are the more visceral things that move people to act. When folks receive personal invitations to exclusive and "invite only" communities, they are intrigued and want in. No one wants to miss out on the fun.

Your message can be as simple as "Hey [name], I've been thinking a lot about [the problem]. I'm trying to bring people together to create [the solution] by doing [the specific activities your community will do]. Would you like to be part of this?"

For example, your message might look like: "Hey Helen! I've been thinking a lot about how hard it is for us to stay connected with school clubs during COVID. I'm trying to bring people together to brainstorm ways to pivot clubs online and troubleshoot the challenges we're facing. I know you're super involved with leading FBLA at your school and am wondering if you'd like to be a part of this?"

I used this strategy last spring while recruiting people for the Youth Organizers Collective, the group of community-minded high school students I brought together around March 2020 to figure how to keep our school club members connected during COVID-19. Helen is a friend I know through FBLA (personal connection!) and immediately RSVP'd to the first YOC Zoom call after receiving my message.

Here are some additional things to note throughout the outreach process:

- Feel free to create an outreach template or use the one above. Copy-paste is your friend; there's no need to start from ground zero every time.
- That said, put people's names in the message! This is one of the easiest ways to personalize it.
- Also, be a human. Do not spam people. If you haven't talked to someone in a while, break the ice by asking them how they are doing or what's on their mind before talking about the community project you're starting.
- If you get a response, reply ASAP. The speed and energy with which you respond is contagious, and signals to the other person how important this is to you. It can get them even more excited about your community.
- Use the snowball strategy. Regardless of whether people respond yes or no to joining your community, ask them if they know others who would be a good fit and deserve an invitation. In this way, anyone can support your work. If someone says no to joining, also understand why so you can iterate on your pitch and better attract the right members. Give existing members a limited number of invitations they can use to invite new ones. It helps them develop a sense of responsibility to grow the community.
- If possible, send messages in batches. After you create your first template, message it to ten people and see how they respond. Are people confused by anything? Did they understand what you're trying to say? Modify your template based on those initial responses and release it to ten more people. As you iterate on your message, you will become more effective in attracting the members you want.

- Finally, if you cannot think of any friends, don't worry! Believe it or not, you can craft intimate asks for people you *don't* personally know. One strategy is to find Instagram accounts aligned with your community's who or why. Look at the followers of those accounts and identify people who fit your ideal community member persona. On big, public social media platforms, people consuming content often lack a way to contribute—they might be looking for something more like what your community offers. Privately DM them and see what they say!

Asks at Scale

Intimate asks are the best place to start for communities of all sizes—but for those who want to grow bigger, asks at scale are key.

Asks at scale are less personal than intimate asks. Instead of one-to-one outreach, it's one-to-many. Outreach becomes a lot more templated and less personalized, which leads to a lower response rate. That said, these types of asks are less time intensive and still lead to quality community members, given effective screening and selection processes.

Some ideas for asks at scale include:

- Posting on social media and running ads (resources allowing)
- Doing takeovers for other organizations' social media platforms
- Promoting in other Slack channels, newsletters, and adjacent communities

These types of asks should clearly and concisely state what your community is about and who you're looking for, so potential members can decide whether it's a good fit. Consider linking your Minimum Viable Canvas, so people can quickly understand your vision for the community. Don't forget to include a call to action, so people know what next steps are. Remember, asks at scale are transactional. If you'd like other spaces to promote your community, you should be willing to do the same! Cross-promoting and supporting mission-aligned communities is a good thing that moves the impact ecosystem forward. For example, #BuiltByGirls, which provides career mentorship for women in STEM, shouting out Girl Genius, an online magazine spotlighting inspiring female leaders in STEM, is a net positive because it helps more young women discover STEM opportunities.

Tagging adjacent communities on social media increases your visibility and builds your credibility as a thought leader. As an added benefit, one of the best ways to deal with off-topic members or people who don't pass your community's selection process is to redirect them to another community better aligned with their interests and qualifications.

All of this is to say, don't mistake asks at scale as a one-time action. Networking consistently across communities is vital!

Selecting People

It's easier to target "the right people" with intimate asks. With asks at scale, engaging your target audience becomes increasingly difficult. When you're broadcasting your community to the public, you can't control the audience.

Many of us have heard the saying, "You're the average of the five people you spend the most time with." The people you surround yourself with matter because you unconsciously adopt both their good and bad characteristics. This is especially so in communities, which reflect the values and actions of the people in it. Vibes, energy, mindsets all easily diffuse across people. Even just one person who loses interest or energy can damage the space. So how do you ensure you end up with the most mission and values-aligned community members?

The answer is simple: have barriers to entry.

Although many prospective members saw your community recruitment post, it doesn't mean each receives an invitation. After you discover people who are interested, weed out the ones who don't share your community's values, aren't excited about your purpose, or don't have bandwidth to fully participate.

To be clear, these people don't necessarily have negative intentions. The community just isn't the right fit, and that's okay! Maybe they didn't read your Minimum Viable Community Canvas before requesting to join. Or maybe they misunderstood what you were trying to say. Either way, you can help them realize why this opportunity isn't a great fit (saving both of you time!) and suggest other communities they can explore.

So how do you create a "barrier to entry" online?

For intimate asks, the barrier to entry is built into the outreach process itself: your community is invite-only. The only way for someone to be invited is through a private DM from a current member who vouches for them. This serves as a built-in screening process.

There are more barriers to entry that can be used individually or combined with intimate asks to strengthen the screening process. They include...

- **An application.** It doesn't need to be pages: three short answer questions, a one-minute video response, or a quick meeting can work! Make a simple rubric to score responses and commit to accepting members who meet a certain score. Application questions should be open-ended and allow people to express their alignment with your community. It's worth noting there are exceptions, and quantitative alignment doesn't always mean a prospective member is the right fit. Trust your intuition as well.
- **Real commitments.** It's easy to sign up for something new, but when most people do, they don't consider the associated responsibilities. Being a good community member requires time and energy. It's helpful to have members define their personal contributions. People may realize they don't have the bandwidth or aren't really *that* passionate about the community, which is 100 percent okay. For example, graduates of the Civics Unplugged (CU) Fellowship who want to join the Civics 2030 community are required to complete a Builder Pledge, a commitment to build a brighter future for humanity. Fellows are invited to reflect on *personal* goals and actions they will take to actualize the community's vision.
- **Demonstrations of skills and energy.** People can make all the commitments they want, but are they able to follow through? If you want to further elevate the barrier to entry, ask people to act on verbal commitments. For example, if someone is interested in helping develop your

community's social media presence, challenge them to create sample posts you can use! If someone would like to help with partnerships, challenge them to come up with a list of mission-aligned organizations to reach out to.

- **An intensive onboarding process.** Finally, the onboarding process itself is a way to weed out people who aren't interested. For example, CU Fellows are required to complete a tech onboarding before the Fellowship starts, where they learn how to use applications like Slack, Zoom, and Notion. If kids are not willing to figure out how the tech platforms work, they will not be a good fit!

As you establish barriers to entry, remember small communities usually have a more robust screening process, and larger ones are laxer. It's both hard to scale barriers of entry (imagine reviewing thousands of detailed applications), and hard to find a lot of people who meet niche and specific requirements. So, think back to your community's original success definition, specifically your desired number of members, and select the barrier to entry(ies) that best serve your needs.

* * *

Onboarding Processes

A solid onboarding process is a screening method for potential community members. Simultaneously, it helps new members gain the context and tools they need to "plug in" to the community from the very beginning. Helping people become familiar with a space increases their ability to engage and take ownership. It helps new members feel welcomed and experience a sense of belonging—both key tenets to a healthy community.

Onboarding is the first sustained interaction you'll have with new community members. An article in *Forbes* describes how we form solid impressions about who people are within the first seven seconds of meeting them. The same goes for forming impressions about a community!

So, what does a sound onboarding process look like?

Onboarding can be anything from a welcome message when people first join explaining the tech platform and where to introduce themselves, to an entire four-month fellowship program. The depth of the process is dependent on the size of your community and expected contributions of each member. Greater contributions require an increased amount of shared context, built during a more complex onboarding phase.

Here are some ideas for things you might include in an onboarding process. Again, there is no "correct" combination of things; choose what makes most sense for your community. Onboarding is a great time to ask members to...

- **Learn how to use the technology.** Especially in digital-first communities, new members need to understand how the community's tech platforms work before they can connect with others. For example, if a community is hosted on Slack and someone has no idea how Slack works, they may not be able to reply in a thread, search for pinned posts, or even introduce themselves in a channel.
- **Craft their introduction.** One of the best ways to kick off the community building process is to get people talking— and there are few things people like to talk about more than themselves.

- In the welcome message, encourage new members to share information that both explains why they are here and introduces themselves outside of the community's immediate context. Knowing someone's history, identity, and personal experiences allows you to gauge why they are here, welcome them, and tailor community experiences to meet their needs.
- You may also designate a "welcoming committee" (which can also just be you) to acknowledge new members who arrive, respond to introductions, and help folks navigate their way around the community. The relationship between the community's creator/main stewards and new members is especially important to help them feel valued.

- **Sign up for an upcoming event**. Clearly identify the places where new members can jump in and experience the community's culture firsthand. Ideally, some of these are icebreaker-type events that maximize one-to-one interaction between members and allow them to engage in meaningful dialogue with as many new people as possible. If you don't want people to lurk, challenge them to sign up for at least one event!

- **Ask questions**. There will no doubt be many questions that surface for folks as they explore the community. Support folks in discovering answers! This can be as simple as creating spaces (like a shared document) for people to "park" their questions so it can be addressed by community moderators or fellow members.

- **Provide feedback on the onboarding process itself**. This allows community members to practice co-creation right from the beginning. Ask members for feedback on onboarding effectiveness, areas of confusion, and other aspects of the process that could be improved. If and when you integrate this feedback, reach out to the community member(s) who introduced the idea and make them aware of their impact.

It may seem overwhelming to do this much just to find your people, but the more work you put into it at the beginning, the more successful your community will be.

Simply put, people are the building blocks of your community. Make sure you have the right folks present through a thoughtful outreach and selection process, and provide members with the knowledge, support, and resources they need to contribute. This is the first step to drive community success.

2.3

TECHNOLOGY

"Online Town, Netflix Party, Discord, ham radio, 3-D printable gifts sent as CAD files, networked printers (the messages printing themselves out like on a Ouija board), meeting up on Figma, meeting up on Mario Party, meeting up on Animal Crossing, meeting up on Minecraft, meeting up on World of Warcraft. My lack of physical presence isn't a limitation, it's a liberation... I don't need my body anymore. I'm enjoying learning how to interact using a new, proprioceptive set of senses. Yes, it's tactile, but I'm not really touching you. Yes, it's visual, but I'm not really seeing you. A phone call feels more intimate than a Zoom call. Doing activities together feels more intimate than talking. The best online interactions I've had don't try to recreate the past, but start with the premise of disembodiment."

—NADIA EGHBAL

Digital communities require digital spaces made possible by... you guessed it, technology! It sounds intuitive, but choosing a tech platform is a step new community builders often gloss over.

When we're in person, the necessity of a good venue seems like a no-brainer. When I served as a state officer for Washington FBLA, we sometimes hosted our state conference at the Meydenbauer Center in Bellevue, WA. While touring the facility, we'd agonize over every microscopic detail, from how students will arrive at the Meydenbauer (How far is it from the hotels? Will people need shuttles?) to how we envision positioning chairs on the conference floor (How many chairs will we need, and how many does the space fit? How do we group them to leave open space for mingling?).

It was important for us to get these questions right because a venue hugely affects the event experience. Real people are going to be in this physical space!

Interestingly enough, we don't apply the same rigor of inquiry to evaluate our digital venues and how they support community members. Online, it's easy to reduce people and space to 2-D things and forget real bodies are attached to the profile pictures you see on screen.

I'm here to remind you real people will take up your digital space, so give them as much thought as you would in-person ones. What do your digital spaces look like and which community tech platform(s) enable them to form?

In the garden metaphor, choosing your technology is akin to choosing a plot of land. Whatever plot of land you choose will become your garden's home for a significant period of time. Whether you choose a skinny plot of land by the highway or an open space next to a community playground will determine which plants show up and how they grow. After all, it's hard to picture neat rows of tulips growing by the road, or a jungle of ferns in someone's backyard garden.

There is no one "best" technology for digital communities —different communities have different needs met by different platforms. The platform you choose is determined by the type of plant you want to "grow," in other words, who you want to show up. Technology creates limitations and opportunities for member interaction, and directly influences your community's culture, processes, and values.

Technology can make or break a community. It's critical to choose wisely.

The good news is, there are many options out there! You're not doing this alone—people have been building digital-first communities for a long time and have created a range of digital venues you can cobble together to meet your needs. Many of these digital venues have been battle-tested by communities that transitioned online due to COVID-19. There is greater accessibility and optionality than ever before. Communities can run with tools that already exist instead of recreating the wheel.

The bad news is there are so many options. It's hard to figure out how a certain platform will affect your community. What does it mean for technology to affect my community's culture and values? And even worse, because the options are so abundant, many community builders default to using "whatever tech platforms everyone else is using," even if it might not be the best fit for their community. *Cue all of the Zoom meetings during COVID-19.*

I was one of those people who used to default to Zoom and didn't fully consider the characteristics of the digital venues each community tech platform creates. That's why this chapter shares some technology options that exist (including and beyond Zoom), how you can choose platform(s) that align most with your community's culture and goals, and how to move between digital venues.

* * *

Technologies to Consider

Community tech platforms serve three core functions: synchronous connection, asynchronous connection, and documentation. At minimum, a community needs at least one of these tools; otherwise, people do not have a place to gather online, much less talk to each other. Thriving communities often cobble together many tech tools that collectively address all three of the core functions because each contributes to the community in a different way.

For each category, I've shared a few key technologies. You may recognize some of the platforms. Others might be new. I focus on technologies that either 1) are widely used by today's youth-led digital-first communities, or 2) embody innovative and promising trends in the industry.

It is important to recognize the list provided is not exhaustive. The community tech space is constantly innovating, and a lot of tools that might not be considered "community tech" can be utilized to enhance your digital community. Per Moore's Law of exponential tech growth, I'm sure this list will become outdated.

Instead, pay attention to the types of digital venues these platforms enable. Let these examples serve as provocations for what is possible and help you *imagine* what an ideal digital venue for your own community might look like.

Whether we're talking about in-person or digital venues, there are ways to use them effectively and ways for them to flop. "Add-ons" can be introduced to digital platforms, like Slack app integrations or interactive PowerPoint software for Zoom presentations. Communities may use the same platform in different ways. Although there are too many variations to address in this chapter, remember these tools can be adjusted to your community's needs.

So, while these recommendations can serve as a foundation for your community tech stack, dig deeper into each platform before making the final decision.

Synchronous

This category describes tech platforms that enable community members to interact "live" online, whether through video, audio, or games. Putting people in the same digital space at the same time creates room for spontaneous interactions. Synchronous activities are more time intensive to organize, but more effective in mimicking the "real-ness" of in-person connection. Live dialogue reminds us real human beings, not just static profile pictures, are behind the screens. It allows people to participate in real time instead of passively consuming content, leading to greater transformational experiences.

Because of all these things, synchronous platforms are a must-have for communities that want intimate relationships between members. For example, if you have a Facebook group or newsletter, the next step might be a Zoom meeting to get to know people better.

While using synchronous technologies, remember it requires more energy from both community builders and members. Especially if "video on" is the norm, people need some degree of preparation (getting camera-ready, being in a quiet location). Spontaneity invites delightful experiences, but also increases the possibility of people colliding in unexpected ways. Setting expectations and having facilitators to manage friction and conflict is key. Synchronous events are best short and sweet!

Some examples of technologies used for synchronous connection include:

- **Video //** Zoom, Facetime, Google Meet, Run The World: Video calls are the most direct alternative to in-person gatherings. You can put faces to names, hear people talk, and observe body language. Small details like people's clothes, background, or even angle of camera, gives us a feel for the person's specific vibe.
    - Zoom is a video-chat platform that makes it easy to have meetings big and small. You've probably used it before, and for good reason. It's super reliable and fast. This is the go-to platform in most communities. Many tools also "level up" Zoom. For example, Nearpod slides increase interactivity by allowing people to collaborate on boards and submit questions. You can even encourage people to "hide self-view" in Zoom, which shifts their attention from themselves to others in the digital space.
    - Because Zoom is also the tool many of us use for work or school, it does carry a more formal, meeting-like

vibe. After all, these calls are literally called Zoom *meetings*. If you're looking for a more social, happy hour vibe, you can start in Zoom and jump into platforms like Gatheround and Glimpse, which make it easy to create short, one-to-one meetings that allow members to connect.

- **Audio** // Clubhouse, phone call, Zoom with cameras off: If your community is Zoomed out (which is totally understandable—sitting in front of a computer all day is draining!), you might experiment with audio-first technologies that allow people to connect in real time while giving them flexibility to be away from their desks. What's cooler, audio even engenders new forms of empathy. Juliana Schroeder, a professor at Berkeley's Haas School of Business, writes audio allows one to "recognize there's this feeling, thinking person behind the words, because you hear those words imbued with their thoughts and feelings in those moments. It happens at the implicit, visceral level and that allows you to humanize the communicator in a way just reading those words does not."

  – Clubhouse is a new drop-in audio platform where people can start voice chat rooms to talk about anything that feels meaningful, or simply listen in.
  – Audio creates a more "chill" vibe. Not seeing a sea of faces staring at you on Zoom can create a non-judgment zone that encourages deeper reflection and vulnerability. For example, a community focused on supporting student mental health during exam season might encourage its members to have their weekly Zoom call with cameras off, while walking out in nature.

- **Virtual world** // Minecraft, Among Us, Animal Crossing: While virtual worlds are more fringe, they are great digital venues to help people bond, even in communities that aren't 100 percent game focused. There's something different about *doing* something together—whether that's singing, dancing, building towers, or finding an imposter—that brings delight into digital spaces.
    - In October 2020, over 400,000 users watched a livestream of Alexandria Ocasio-Cortez playing Among Us on Twitch. *Vox* describes AOC as "a winning Twitch personality, ranking alongside the best of them; she laughed, she yelled, she gasped, and viewers did the same alongside her, all while she engaged with people on important issues" such as directing them to I Will Vote and plugging the Biden-Harris ticket.
    - Minecraft is a video game that allows players to create and break apart various blocks to build three-dimensional worlds. It allows members to articulate a shared vision for the future and work together to realize that vision in the digital realm. Building something together is therapeutic and creates a sense of ownership among participants.

Asynchronous

This category describes tools that enable community members to interact while *not* present in the same digital space at the same time. Think message boards where someone might post a message, and an hour later, their friend pops in the chat, sees their message, and responds. In a time when people are getting "Zoomed out," asynchronous platforms serve as a kinder collaboration method that meets people based on their energy level.

The fact is most people can't be on Zoom meetings 24/7. Some people, like me, need to recharge by spending time alone. Asynchronous platforms give community members a way to stay connected without the need to hop on another Zoom.

While synchronous touchpoints like Zoom events may seem like the "highlights" of your community, asynchronous technology is where you can continue the conversation. Synchronous experiences represent meticulously planned day trips with friends into the city, where there's pressure to be fun and take lots of pretty photos for Instagram. Asynchronous ones are all the times when your friend just comes over to hang out. It's where the grounded, joyful, and easy moments that bridge the highlights take place. The repetition and stability that asynchronous platforms provide are key to developing community.

To be clear: asynchronous tech cannot replace the "face-to-face" connection of synchronous platforms. Certain (complex, vulnerable, nuanced) things are not meant to be communicated over text, so don't! That said, synchronous and asynchronous technologies build off each other's strengths in amazing ways, and asynchronous doesn't mean boring. You can be intentional with design choices such as emojis, lower case text, and language to craft the community you want.

Some examples of technologies used for asynchronous connection include:

- **Multi-channel chat** // Slack, Discord
  - Slack is *the* asynchronous community building platform to explore. Originally designed for start-ups

and distributed teams, it's a popular chat platform that can be used on both mobile and desktop to send messages to select people, groups, or the community as a whole. Furthermore, there are tons of extensions that customize Slack for your community. For example, HeyTaco! is a tool that allows community members to shout out others by giving them tacos, a form of digital community currency. Other tools, like Donut, match people in a certain Slack channel for custom icebreakers.

- Discord can be thought of as "Slack for gamers." The two platforms share many of the same functionalities, such as varying sized group chats, channels to organize discussions, and threads to respond to others' comments. Discord also allows for easy customization of someone's experience in the community based on their role (think how this can be applied to onboarding processes!) and voice channels for built-in audio-first collaboration.

- **Social media** // Instagram, Facebook, 2Swim
  - People have been gathering on social media for years. Social media can be a synchronous platform, but usually acts as an asynchronous one. Most people spend time on Instagram crafting posts and passively scrolling, not hosting Instagram Lives.
  - While it's hard for community to be an Instagram page (too many people → people feel anonymous), private social media group chats are a common asynchronous space for budding communities (Instagram chats, Facebook groups). Social media sparks loose bonds that can be moved into smaller, private communities for deeper relationship building.

- Finally, many new "social-media-like" platforms are popping up to address pitfalls of traditional social media, such as the pressure to virtue signal—communicate a good character by publicly expressing a moral viewpoint—and compare likes. For example, 2Swim is a social platform that doesn't have posts with likes, but rather private communities and ephemeral messaging where virtue signaling isn't effective. You can't virtue signal to close friends, who judge you by your everyday actions, not words.

Documentation

Communities need a way to stay on the same page.

This category describes tools that enable communities to document processes, learn collaboratively, and coordinate members. The structures and practices of your community need to live *somewhere*, and writing it down is often one of the best practices to create value and build community. Documentation platform(s) shared between members and stewarded by the community are instrumental in organizing information and making it accessible.

As you read through the platforms below, remember content does not equal community. Content is simply something your community can gather around, or something that comes *from* your community. Community cannot develop just with a documentation platform; you'll need one of the synchronous or asynchronous tools to have enough touch points for relationships to form!

Some examples of technologies used for documentation include:

- **Website** // Wix, Wordpress, Squarespace: Websites are landing pages where people stumble upon your community and learn more about what you do. They also host information for current members; communities might link whitepapers or event recordings on the website, crowdsource blog articles, or post a calendar of upcoming events. Drag and drop website builders like Wix make it easy for anyone to set up a professional-looking, well-designed website in a couple hours.

- **Newsletter** // Substack, email: Newsletters play an essential role in curating information—so much exists on the internet it's hard to make sense of things. Communities often form around newsletters, especially if its content explores a unique theme.
  - Pre-community: Newsletters show potential members what your community is about and demonstrate the community builder's passion behind the topic.
  - Post-community: Newsletters distill what goes on in the community, share highlights, shout out members, circulate key insights, and serve as public reflection. It keeps everyone on the same page! Especially in youth-centered communities, members' engagement will ebb and flow (think: everyone disappears during finals season). Newsletters create a no-pressure way for people to stay in the loop and jump back in whenever they can.

- **File storage** // Google Drive, Dropbox: Having a place to work on and store shared documents is critical for collaboration. Imagine having to edit a Word doc and email out the newest version to everyone in your community... no, thanks. Google Drive is the go-to tool. It's secure, fast, free, and updates documents in real time. The majority of young people are already on Google Drive due to school, making the barrier to entry virtually nonexistent.

- **Notion**: Notion is an incredible notetaking and document management platform that allows community members to organize and collaborate in new ways. It's versatile, user-friendly, aesthetic, and a great way to store everything from whitepapers to member directories to weekly meeting dashboards. There is a learning curve to Notion, especially if your members are used to Google Drive, but it's a platform worth adopting. Many technologies have certain Notion functionalities, but none integrates them like Notion does. For example, Notion includes functions found in...

  - Google Drive—Create, share, comment, and collaborate in documents.

  - Airtable—Organize complex information using databases, use functions like relations and rollups to connect data between tables.

  - Trello—Generate tasks, assign them to members, and add relevant information in a Kanban-style board.

* * *

Which Platform(s) Should I Choose?

At the end of the day, technology is a means to an end. It can always be swapped out or changed, so don't get overwhelmed with choosing the "perfect" one. Make the best decision you can using the three principles below, get feedback from your community members, and move forward. Just as you don't want to get stuck in the outreach phase, don't get stuck in the "find a tech platform" phase. You can always transition to a new platform down the road.

1. Mold technology to your people, not the other way around

Technology exists to serve your community. When you select your community tech, consider how your chosen platform(s)...

- **Engage people on platforms they're already using**: Depending on the size and demographics of community members, different platforms will best suit your needs. For example, if you have a 300-person community, it doesn't make sense to use an Instagram group chat (it doesn't even accommodate that many people)! It might be fine to start a group chat with twenty people, but as you grow, move into more robust platforms like Slack. Meanwhile, if you're building a community for Gen Zers, it probably doesn't make sense to use a Facebook group.
- **Supercharge what your people do together**: What is the *why* behind your community? If you have a community of beginners who practice yoga together, an audio-first platform may not be the best choice. How will people know what yoga movements to do? Similarly, if your community organizes voter registration drives, doing so in an Instagram group chat seems unprofessional and disorganized. Resources get lost, emojis/memes distract from serious questions, and people scroll through important content in the same headspace as when checking in on

what their friends ate for lunch... Instead of Instagram, you might opt for hosting recorded sessions on Zoom, using Slack for offline collaboration, and a shared Notion workspace with all the training materials.

2. Technology should reflect your values

Every piece of technology inspires and perpetuates certain values. For example, Google Classroom is built in a way that values hierarchy and centralization of power. We can see this in how a teacher has full control of the classroom. They are the only ones who can post materials and assignments. Students can only DM the teacher and not each other. The values embedded in whatever technology you select will emerge in your community as well.

If your community values...

- **Inclusion**, think about using platforms that require less internet bandwidth (WhatsApp vs Instagram chat) or platforms offered on both mobile and desktop devices (Zoom vs Remo, another video conferencing app). Things like closed captioning, image descriptions, and profile pronouns can also make a digital space more inclusive.
- **Safety**, consider how your chosen platform protects the privacy of community members. Do people understand what they are signing up for and how their data will be used? Platforms like Clubhouse prevent recording conversations. Zoom asks for permission to record and gives folks the option to turn off their camera or leave. What affordances does your chosen platform provide, and are they enough?

It's important to note a technology can reflect multiple values, and multiple technologies can reflect the same value. A lot of it comes down to *how* you use a platform as well.

3. Don't let technology overcomplicate

All of these platforms look super cool. It's tempting to use all of them. Remember technology should enhance connections and enable you and your members to do *more* than before. If a platform has a net negative impact (confuses people, makes documents even harder to find), remove or don't use it!

Technology should make life easier. Two things to keep in mind:

- **Choose your platform(s) and commit**. Just like how we wouldn't recommend splitting your garden into two different plots of land or moving your garden to a new location every two weeks, don't move the people in your community too much either. While you should be willing to pivot and experiment with the technologies you use, every decision should be intentional. Give the current platform(s) a real chance before you move on! For example, it wouldn't make sense to use both Slack and Discord or alternate between them weekly. Both asynchronous technologies serve the same purpose. It will only disperse energy and confuse members on where they should show up.
- **Start simple**. Certain technologies are incredible but can take time to adopt. Depending on the length of your onboarding process and how involved the average community member will be, simpler platforms may be more

user-friendly while still giving you the functions you need. Notion is amazing, but not if you only see people twice a month and everyone already uses Google Drive!

* * *

What If I Change My Mind?

Given communities evolve, don't be alarmed if the tech platform(s) you use evolve as well. Your community might adopt a new platform if something has changed about your people or mission, and the current platform no longer meets the collective's needs. Or, you might experiment with a new platform with potential to help your community better realize its mission. Simply moving to a flashier platform because "everyone else is using it" is not a good reason!

It's normal to lose some members in the process of platform transition. Maybe some folks were disengaged and don't realize the move is happening, get lost in the process, or the new platform isn't the best fit for them. It's just like moving plants from one garden to another—some plants might die while getting uprooted or get lost along the trip. Your garden won't look 100 percent the same after you move.

Here are ways you can support community members and minimize people who fall through the cracks during the transition:

- **Articulate why you're moving**: Identify the needs of your community not being met by the current tech platform. What functionalities or values are your members looking for? Go the extra mile to explain to members why and how a new platform can help.

- **Learn about the new platform**: Become an expert in the new option so YOU can guide people through it. You should know the strengths and weaknesses of the platform in order to make a well-informed decision on whether this transition will better serve members.
- **Engage your community**: Create a proposal and seek out community buy-in to decide if and how you should change platforms. This practice creates feedback channels and helps members feel a sense of ownership and responsibility for the community's future. Thoughtfully listen to and incorporate feedback you receive, then go back to members and show how their feedback was used!
- **Run experiments**: Test the new platform with a small group. This can happen simultaneously with the proposal and feedback process. It's useful for members to experience what the new platform feels like so they can provide specific feedback on why they do or do not like it, and whether it fits the community's vibe.
- **Give advance notice**: Once the decision to transition tech platforms is made, give members adequate advance notice. This is especially important if your decision affects every member (such as moving the core asynchronous community from Slack to Discord). If you're changing to Google Meet instead of Zoom, or moving your Notion dashboard into weekly newsletters, less preparation is needed from members.
- **Offer support**: During the transition phase, make sure every member knows what is going on and where they can find support. Troubleshooting sessions, small group

demos, and a parking lot for questions can support members throughout this process.

There is an abundance of digital platforms and tools that can be used to cultivate online communities; only a couple have been referenced in this chapter. Dedicate time to exploring and experimenting with these technologies! Consult your members in the process.

Ultimately, just like your plot of land can make or break a garden, your tech platform(s) can make or break digital communities. Choose wisely now to prevent unnecessary confusion down the road. If you do need to pivot, that's completely fine—just make sure every decision is intentionally made.

2.4

CREATE SPACE

—

"If you actually care about the kinds of interactions that people are having in this space, as a governance matter, then you would try to maximize an architecture that looks more like Reddit and groups than you would build for 'anybody gets to come.'

It's just another way of understanding that when you go to the library, you don't go to a park. What is the desirability of having lots of open park-like space (where anybody gets to do whatever they want) as opposed to libraries and museums? The designers of these spaces can make choices."

—TRACEY MEARES

You now have the supplies you need to build your community: the people who give your community spirit and the tech platform(s) to host them on. The next step involves creating guardrails that allow people to show up as their whole selves.

Imagine this: you're a new student at a big middle school. When you walk into the lunchroom, you notice the "popular girls" sitting at a table together. The table is really big, and there is clearly an open seat. There's room for another person! You wonder why no one has claimed it yet and quickly have your answer. Every time someone not from their clique nears, all the girls openly glare at the intruder. Even though there is a seat, would you say there is "space" at the table? No!

There is an important distinction between what was discussed in the previous chapter, choosing a platform, and this chapter, creating space on the platform. Just because you're hosting a Zoom meeting with "lots of space" because there's no attendee limit doesn't mean people can or will show up if you didn't design the space to be inclusive and welcoming.

Being welcomed into a space isn't just about availability, it's about being desired for your gifts, contributions, and simply who you are.

Remember: Community building is a space-making practice. You might've heard before the need to create "safe spaces" or "brave spaces." Without space, people are not able to communicate their needs or contribute their gifts. We miss out on the ideas, feelings, questions, and provocations that arise when people are encouraged to show up fully.

In the worst-case scenario, people will not show up at all—and when individuals start withholding their contributions, the community itself loses its ability to attain its purpose.

This dilemma poses the question: How might we design digital spaces where members are seen and accepted fully, both in their strengths but also in their flaws? How do we explain to people *how* they should show up?

Creating space doesn't happen by magic. Even if the popular girls at the lunch table were neutral (they could've just ignored everyone who approached), people probably still wouldn't have mustered up the courage to take that empty seat. In our communities, we need to do better than neutral. We need to actively bring people into the fold and create opportunities for them to step in. This requires forethought and awareness of those around us.

In this chapter, I will show you how rules and facilitation make that possible. Rules offer guidelines that explain how a community will achieve its goals and embody its values. Facilitation helps community builders hold space for empathy, tension, and growth, both between individual members and between the collective and the world. Both practices increase *joyful belonging*: time spent in communities of great connection, meaning, and depth.

In a world marked by rising loneliness, what do people need more than spaces of joyful belonging? And what do communities need more than people who are confident enough to provide feedback, share ideas, and take initiative to push the collective forward?

Rules and facilitation are essential design choices that make your community more effective in achieving your goals.

* * *

Rules

Rules are critical to holding space.

Just think about it—we constantly lament social media for being toxic and unwelcoming. Few people like polarizing perspectives, curse words in ALL CAPS, mis/disinformation, and inconsistent suspension of accounts. Where do all these problems stem from? Insufficient rules. We have rules that are arbitrary and poorly enforced, rules that aren't enough to guarantee a civil conversation, or simply no rules at all.

Without rules, digital space becomes a free-for-all. Any individual can take as much space as they want, use it however they desire, and co-opt the community for their own benefit.

If you read the Community Canvas, you might remember the Membership Rules section. The Canvas emphasizes the need to set expectations for members, so everyone knows how they are expected to contribute (and can choose not to, by leaving the community). There are three categories of expectations:

- **Etiquette**: How community members treat each other and the community infrastructure. How do individuals embody the community's values and put them into action? For example, a community might ask its members to "follow the golden rule."
- **Commitment**: Just like how citizenship comes with responsibilities, membership does too. What duties do members have and how do they contribute? For example, a community might decide active members must attend a monthly community gathering.
- **Accountability**: Consequences must be clearly communicated in order for a rule to be taken seriously. For example, a community might use a three-strike system to remove members. On the first strike, members receive a verbal correction or formal warning, followed by a temporary mute. On the second strike... (you get the idea!)

A set of rules in your community communicates expectations around how people should act. Rather than being a nuisance or inconvenience, they help members interact in meaningful, productive ways.

Rules are not rocket science. On some level, we all know what it looks like to treat something with respect. We want to take responsibility for our actions, live up to our commitments, and be trusted by peers. To this point, rules are intuitive. You're not telling people things they don't know; you're simply surfacing the community's wisdom, writing it down somewhere, and pointing to it over time.

It's also worth noting most people *want* to comply with the rules. You just need to tell them what the rules are and do so in a way that legitimizes both you as the community builder and the community itself. Humans don't have the best memories, so if we don't revisit our rules enough, we will forget them—even if we didn't have ill intent. When you have rules and treat people like they're upstanding community members who follow them, they will be more likely to do so!

Even if you think you don't need rules for your community for whatever reason (size, type of people, nature of topic), it is important you do. You never know what will happen as your community evolves, and it's helpful to have processes in place to deal with conflict, harm, uncomfortable moments, and other points of tension, if and when they arise.

Hopefully I've convinced you to join team rules. Let's get to it.

How to Create Rules

When creating rules, it's a lot easier to work backward from your end goal: the type of digital space you want to create. What are the conditions of that space, and what rules create those conditions? Mapping rules to your community's design objectives ensures rules are not solely created to signal power. *Designing Our Intentions*, a resource created by the Stanford d.school to set group intentions for digital spaces, recommends the following steps:

1. **Reflect**. What's a moment where you've had a transformational conversation? When did you feel safe, included, and understood? We assume this environment is the type of space you want to replicate in your community.
2. **Excavate**. What conditions/behaviors/agreements were in place to shape that moment? What unspoken norms were followed by the people involved, including yourself? What processes were present to help the group navigate tricky terrain?
3. **Generate**. Based on your answers above, what intentions might be helpful for community members as they work together to create space for each other?

Note how this process trusts community members to have a vision for the space they want to see. Rules are something that emerge from the collective to meet people's needs—not something to protect the power of those "at the top."

It's wise to harness members' energy and imagination to envision an aspirational community space. Everyone has had different moments where they felt safe, included, and understood. It is a community builder's responsibility to ensure diverse experiences and perspectives are represented among the group who crafts the initial set of rules. If you're the sole person writing the first draft, consult your members as much as possible.

By ensuring members feel like *they* contribute to foundational rules, you'll increase legitimacy, buy-in, and adoption down the road.

That said, it's easy to get carried away with rules and let them evolve into some complex, unintelligible mass of words. Just look at the US tax code! As you crowdsource rules and write them down, remember to prioritize clarity and conciseness. You don't need to include *every* suggestion, and when in doubt, simple rules are better! Rules already aren't the most exciting documents to read, and having multiple pages only makes it more dispiriting.

Try to condense and consolidate when possible. Use the rule of threes, a writing principle that suggests things that come in threes are inherently funny, satisfying, and more effective than any other number. Acronyms, bullet points, and short phrases also make rules more digestible.

How to Organize and Present Your Rules

How you package and deliver the rules to your community is equally important as what the rules are.

For example, consider the word "rule." To be honest, "rules" don't give me the best vibe—it reminds me of curfews, hierarchy, and other frustratingly rigid processes at school like raising my hand and requesting permission from the teacher to use the bathroom. I (like many of my peers) prided myself on being a rule-breaker at school, which is why I'm guessing we usually don't call them "rules" in our clubs and organizations. They'd just be broken!

Instead, the rules we discussed earlier can take on many forms, such as code of conduct, community guidelines, group norms, or something else entirely. Each form gives off a different vibe and serves a different purpose. Whereas "group norms" sounds more chill and might be a good fit for a fun, self-organized online book club, "code of conduct" sounds more corporate and might better fit a professional student business organization.

Some common ways rules are presented, from least to most complex, include...

- **Group norms.** If your community is smaller or time-bound, simple group norms might be more effective than an elaborate set of guidelines. Norms are rules of behavior that naturally emerge between members, like arriving on time or stepping up, stepping back. Write them down!
- **Community guidelines.** If you have a medium-sized community and aren't sure how to organize rules, this is a good default. Whereas norms are values-based and open to interpretation, guidelines are comprehensive and enforced by community facilitators/moderators. As a result, guidelines hold greater weight and include tangible consequences when broken.
- **Code of conduct.** A code of conduct describes specific ways in which members should/shouldn't act, such as "do not type anything that is spammy, inappropriate, or rude." It's especially helpful for larger, execution-oriented communities building significant things together, such as an open-source project or online conference.
- **Constitution.** This structure is one of the most robust and comprehensive ways to present rules. It's best suited for communities with complex governance structures, especially if you're managing shared funds or other resources together.

Regardless of how you choose to package your rules, remember accessibility is key. Members should easily find your rules and understand them. Consider using one of the documentation tools mentioned in the previous chapter to store your rules in a public place, like a new member onboarding guide or the #help channel in Slack. In real life, this is the equivalent of posting your rules on a bulletin board in your community's gathering place.

Seeing the rules over and over reminds people to use them!

How to Enforce Your Rules

Creating rules is relatively easy, compared to enforcing them. It is a difficult balance to strike—how can we be understanding of community members' mistakes, while maintaining rigorous honesty about the harm they have caused?

The good news is people have already identified a set of mutually agreeable rules before harm happened. More complex rules like a constitution or code of conduct often includes things like what actions constitute a strike and the consequences at each level, such as verbal warnings, temporary mute/probation, and removal from the community. In these scenarios, simply point back to your rules and follow the process laid out. Let the rules serve as an "objective" document to hold people accountable.

While "softer rules" like community guidelines and group norms usually don't lay out processes for conflict resolution, holding people accountable remains equally important. As a community builder, one of your core responsibilities is to create a space where people feel safe, included, and understood. When a guideline or norm is violated, consider not only how to deal with the situation at hand, but how your response (or lack of) indicates your values.

Especially at the beginning of your community building journey, your actions set a precedent that affects the community's behavior and expectations.

Two practices are useful when enforcing rules: 1) acknowledge one has been broken, and 2) hold people accountable kindly, but firmly. Depending on the rule broken and the frequency, you might address them by...

- **Reach out to the person privately.** If the violation is a first-time offense, this is a good choice. Maybe the member is new to the community and was not aware of the rules. Give people the benefit of the doubt!
- **Give the person a public warning.** Calling out unacceptable behavior conveys to the rest of the community the rules are taken seriously. It's a powerful way to acknowledge any harm caused by the person's actions and restore space. The challenge, and what makes this process intricate, is how to call out the behavior while calling in the person. How might we move beyond an accusation and reaction, and create space for reflection and change? Consider leading with the personal impacts of someone's actions (Mary, when you did [x], it made me feel...), suggesting new practices folks might adopt (Another way to make your point might be...), and resources where they can learn more ([x] is a helpful resource to learn more about this issue).

Remember: "enforcing rules" isn't one and done. It's an ongoing, infinite conversation—and one you are going to have to accept and get comfortable with in order to build communities.

Are there weekly check-ins to help your most active members reflect on the expectations they've set for each other and the group? Regular action to remove inactive members from the community? Embedding accountability into your community's processes makes it less awkward. Instead of sparking nerve-wracking conversations, rules become a tool any member can lean on to help themselves and those around them show up as their best selves.

If you struggle with enforcing your community's rules, also consider the root cause of why members are breaking them. Are the rules unclear? Does the design of your tech platform(s) make it hard to hold people accountable? Is your leadership not modeling rules and expectations? It is valuable to take a step back and consider what the situation says about your community and leadership team.

* * *

Facilitation

While rules are by no means static, they are slower to change and may be clunky to apply in the moment. For example, if you're on a Zoom call and someone says something that breaks a group norm, it's not typical for another member to say, "Hey! Didn't you read the group norms list? You just broke bullet number five!"

To carry out and apply rules in those moments, communities rely on skilled facilitators. Facilitators help groups stay focused, hold space for everyone to participate, and ultimately enable groups of members to accomplish more than they would have been able to. If you've been to an in-person conference, you can think of facilitation as the role that panel moderators or workshop leaders play. While you don't need a facilitator at every event, it makes sense to have one present when you want members to accomplish a certain goal (reach agreement, create new insights, build something together) during the event time frame.

I like to think of facilitators as **process guides**—they steward the *process* of working together cooperatively and effectively. Facilitators don't act as participants or have all the answers. They can't impose an outcome on the group. In my small backyard garden at home, my dad is the "facilitator." He's not the one doing the planting of seeds, but rather guides me and my younger sisters to do so. He helps us remember the end goal, find tasks that play to our strengths, and asks questions to help us move in the right direction (What do you want to plant? What did the directions on the seed packet say? What supplies or information are we missing?). There's no way for my dad to be 100 percent sure the garden will flourish, but having him there definitely increases that likelihood.

Sue Atchley Ebaugh said, "The greatest gift we can give one another is rapt attention to one another's existence." This is the gift facilitators bring to the community. By listening with rapt attention, asking good questions, and making observations, facilitators *see* community members fully and encourage them to lean in and contribute their gifts, thus helping bring about better outcomes from the group interaction.

In order for facilitators to be effective, they play a couple roles that might not be intuitive. Specifically, facilitators are...

- **Multi-partial**. Facilitators are curious about and pay attention to all opinions from members, including those not expressed. They separate themselves from their own biases and try to bring as many perspectives into the conversation as possible, even playing devil's advocate if people are being overly diplomatic or agreeable. This ensures even if a perspective isn't represented by the majority, it is considered and valued.
- **Provocateurs**. Facilitators help members challenge status quo beliefs and shift dialogue toward personal experiences, feelings, and critical thinking. It's natural for strangers to prompt surface level "how's the weather?" questions when they first meet. Without a facilitator, members may not feel comfortable going deeper. By asking challenging questions and helping groups sit with tension, facilitators empower members to gain ownership over their dialogue.
- **Process guides**. While facilitators can model how to do something for members, they are not another participant. Facilitators should not contribute the majority of the discussion, "solve" all the challenges groups come across, or always have the answer. Certain things, like taking a stance or talking too much, can compromise a facilitator's ability to be multi-partial and hold space for *all* members.

In the early stages of your community, the facilitator will likely be you, the community builder! The person who calls a community together is naturally expected to catalyze conversation and progress. You might find yourself starting to mirror some of the traits above.

As your community scales and members develop a better understanding of the community's rules and culture, more people may step up to facilitate. Facilitating is one of the best ways to empower new leaders and help members take ownership of community experiences. Provide members with the knowledge, resources, and support they need to facilitate. Every member should be able to create the spaces they want to see, and facilitation is a big part of that!

Key Facilitation Techniques

So, what does facilitation look like in action?

In a Zoom meeting, facilitators may act as hosts: welcoming people into the call, keeping an eye on the chat, operating the technologies on the backend, summarizing what the group has said, and moving the group along. In an asynchronous space, like Slack, facilitators play less of a hands-on role and may serve as more of a moderator: pinning posts, tagging people to respond to questions, redirecting to new channels if necessary, and making sure posts follow community guidelines.

On any platform, facilitators introduce questions and provocations that prompt members to reflect and invite engagement.

Most people don't "naturally facilitate" and can find it challenging. It's probably not your personality to be multi-partial, a provocateur, or a process guide. That is completely normal! We are often invited into spaces as participants, not guides, and haven't had the chance to flex our facilitation muscles yet.

While facilitation is nerve-wracking and a skill that requires a lot of practice to develop, it can also be incredibly rewarding. Facilitation is one of the simplest and most effective ways for *any* member to shape where the community is headed.

More importantly, facilitation is a skill set that can be learned and practiced. Some of the key skills to practice include...

- **Active listening.** Listening with rapt attention helps members feel understood. To determine whether you're actively listening, notice what you're thinking about when someone else is talking. Are you taking in and processing what they are saying, or already thinking of your talking points and response? Active listening helps people feel seen by...
  - Mirroring: reflecting back to a community member what they said. It's generally used to ensure understanding: "What I'm hearing you say is... is that right?" This gives members a chance to clarify or add on to what they meant. Especially if someone keeps going in circles or restating a point, mirroring can help them feel heard while moving the conversation forward.
  - Summarizing: helping tie together various points into a coherent thought. This practice is especially helpful when there is information overload or when the group is jumping around. The facilitator can summarize, identify points that were skipped, and help the group return to what is most important.
- **Asking good questions.** Questions are a fundamental facilitation tool. The right questions can move a group toward understanding and equal participation. More often than not, people *want* to share where their opinions and feelings come from. Good questions help people connect on a deeper, more vulnerable level that builds trust.
  - At all times, facilitators should try to surface questions the *community* has and let members guide the discussion.

- Asking open-ended questions may appear intuitive. In addition to open-endedness, it's important to consider factors such as:
  - Question length: Questions should remain concise and not interrupt the flow of the conversation. If your question requires a monologue of context, it's not the best fit.
  - Embedded assumptions: Questions should not guide community members toward your answer. Avoid leading questions ("Don't you think that...") or providing a menu of options ("Do you think climate change exists because of x, y, or z?")
  - Accessibility: Every community member should understand and be able to respond to the question. For example, if you have a nontechnical community, it doesn't make sense to pose a coding question. This is why it's helpful to connect questions to personal experiences. People know a lot about and are great at speaking about themselves.
- **Making observations.** Observations help community members feel recognized and acknowledged, beyond the content of what they are saying. For example, facilitators may observe things like...
  - Body language: Yes, body language exists on Zoom! For example, if someone is frowning a lot or looks confused, it's powerful for the facilitator to send them a DM asking if everything is okay and what help they need.
  - Power dynamics: Power dynamics often revolve around who is speaking and how much. Sometimes,

language barriers or tech challenges can prevent certain members from fully participating. In these scenarios, facilitators can intentionally create space for these people (e.g., "I noticed our participants from Algeria have not spoken yet. Would anyone like to share their thoughts?").

- Appreciate vulnerability: Just like facilitators mirror content, it's also important to mirror emotions expressed. Sharing takes a lot of courage. It's great to shout people out for that, especially if vulnerability is something you're trying to encourage. Appreciation is as simple as saying, "Thank you for sharing that with us" or "I noticed a lot of [emotion] in your voice as you were talking about x. It seems like x is very important to you."

Again, rules and facilitation rarely come naturally. These practices might feel uncomfortable at first, but you'll move up the conscious competence ladder with practice. Encourage feedback from community members along the way—for example, there might be a hand signal members can use to indicate "ouch" or "slow down." An anonymous space for folks to put concerns about your facilitation leads to authentic feedback.

Real, challenging feedback from both participants, observers, and fellow facilitators has been essential in my own development. This is coming from someone who used to *never* practice deep listening (always too busy preparing my response to "look good"), who now feels confident mirroring and summarizing in dialogues. If I can do it, you can too.

Ultimately, space isn't something magically afforded by the technology your community uses or the fact you're online.

It's something you'll have to work to create! You're not always going to get it right and it's okay to learn as you go. Having positive intentions is the first step. You got this!

2.5

FACILITATE
TRANSFORMATION

—

*"If you inherently long for something, become it first. If
you want gardens, become the gardener. If you want
love, embody love. If you want mental stimulation,
change the conversation. If you want peace, exude
calmness. If you want to fill your world with artists,
begin to paint. If you want to be valued, respect your
own time. If you want to live ecstatically, find the
ecstasy within yourself. This is how to draw it in, day
by day, inch by inch."*

—VICTORIA ERICKSON

It is a basic human need to grow and evolve.

Just like the plants in our garden, if we are not growing,
we are dying—and the reason we grow is because we have
something of value to give. Few things are more critical to
our well-being than always learning, expanding our sense of

self, and contributing to the world around us. We constantly search for experiences that allow for a process of self-discovery, to figure out who we are. These experiences are often found in community.

Cowell College's motto, "The pursuit of truth in the company of friends," perfectly describes what we experience in community: We're pursuing our why together, and there's a pleasantness to it. Collaboration instead of competition. We get to show up as our whole selves and engage in conversations that make us feel alive. In this space, we have the greatest chance to experience self-transcendence, a connection with deeper meaning and purpose.

Opportunities for self-transcendence are critical, because people become obsessed with and loyal to the experiences that transform them.

If we aren't constantly leveling up many parts of the community and the people within them, we will not provide transformative experiences that keep members coming back and drive them to *give* back. Think of officer elections for a school club. Few candidates say, "I don't contribute much to this community, and it hasn't changed me at all, but I want to run for office." Instead, people say, "I'm running today because [club] has influenced my life in [ways], and I want to make it even better and help more students access this opportunity."

If you filled out the Community Canvas, you may have noticed *Shared Experiences* is one of the seventeen themes. It explores questions like, "How do the individual experiences connect to the community's overall goals?" and "How are shared experiences organized?" An entire section of the Canvas (the upper red section) is even titled "Experience" and is all about rituals, traditions, events, and stories.

The Canvas highlights the necessity of transformative experiences to facilitate human flourishing. On both an individual and collective level, these experiences allow us to...

- **Inspire buy-in.** Transformative events catalyze change. The ship is moving, which creates a sense of urgency for folks to get onboard and make history with the community. By tapping into people's sense of FOMO (no one wants to miss out on an opportunity for growth!), transformation serves as a forcing function for people to actively participate.
- **Evolve and adapt to change.** Transformative events "level up" both individual beliefs and community processes in response to changes in and out of the community. If a community doesn't constantly evolve it's *who* and *why*, it will fail to attract new members and create impact. One of the easiest ways to ensure a community doesn't remain static is to create transformative experiences for the people in it.

Our question remains: What are transformative experiences, and how do we create them?

It's important to remember at the most basic level, transformation is about the individual. People are the smallest units of community. When individuals change for the better, how they show up in the community (the character, strengths, and vibe they bring) also changes for the better.

Imagine your community cares about climate action, and you'd like to encourage members to eat vegan to reduce their carbon footprint. After getting appropriate buy-in from community members, you decide to email your community a few articles about veganism and update your website to reflect this new priority—but don't actually work with individuals to make lifestyle changes. Nothing happens. For real transformation, people need to engage with ideas. You might have one-to-one conversations with members about the health benefits of veganism, or host events where people shop for vegan ingredients and create recipes together.

This chapter shares strategies to facilitate transformation for community members, and by extension, your community. It discusses...

- **Events**—how *every* community event can become a transformational experience.
- **Learning experiences**—how cohort-based courses and short, tiny, exclusive experiences make learning exciting.
- **Rituals**—how they create space for new narratives and inspire behavior change.

Remember: Truly transformational experiences are not just nice-to-have, but essential to the longevity of your community!

* * *

How to Make Events Transformational

It's not a coincidence when many of us consider how to create transformative experiences, we think of hosting events. Our lives are punctuated by events. They are the highlights!

Project Exchange's Digital Exchange Program (DEP) hosts optional Saturday events that range from movie nights to world fairs. These events engage students, foster connections between them, and meet the fluctuating needs of every DEP cohort. Interestingly, a number of students don't "graduate" from the DEP by completing the curriculum but choose to stay involved because of Saturday events.

That said, more events are not always better.

After all, events can become a chore! If you've been to school Zoom meetings, you know how draining it is. You're sitting there, not really engaging, listening to the teacher drone on about something you'll probably never use. It's the same thing day-in and day-out. You're counting down the minutes until the clock says 3:10 p.m. so you can click "leave meeting" as fast as humanly possible...

In the *Art of Gathering*, Priya Parker writes, "A gathering's blandness is a symptom of disease. And what is the disease? That the gathering makes no effort to do what the best gatherings do: transport us to a temporary alternative world." Often, events are an escape: a space for us to do things that aren't a duty, but a pleasure. Other times, the promise of events is to create space for collective dreaming and realizing components of the world we want to see. Being transported to a different space allows us to shift our perspective on what is possible and bring that back to the "real world" after events conclude.

So, what differentiates a transformative event from a bland one?

An event is made transformative when someone is rewarded with a new experience that changes their perspective on the world. People want to feel like meaningful participants. If you invite someone to an event, they should be able to impact how the event goes, even if it's just in some small way. By engaging members as co-creators, members learn how to replicate these events in new situations both in and out of the community, modifying structure and adjusting processes to make it relevant.

Civics Unplugged does a great job of organizing events that put community members in the driver's seat. Their events include...

- **Juntos**—intimate, mutual support groups of about eight Builders in the CU community who gather weekly to set goals, hold each other accountable, and discuss whatever feels meaningful. The agenda is always open; people can introduce agenda items such as sanity checking projects, getting feedback on important decisions, and jamming on ideas.

- **Treks**—a dialogue series where community members participate in free-flowing discussion around any topic meaningful to CU and building the future, from "regenerative space" to "contemporary chaos." Treks are lightly structured into three sections: word association, questions and provocations, and reflections and application—all driven by participants.

- **Unmasterclasses**—a lecture series where community members share their passion around a topic. It's the opposite of a traditional masterclass, where the lecturer is expected to be an expert. Here, there is no such expectation. Instead, lecturers give a short presentation to establish a common starting point, which enables genuine knowledge exchange where both participants and the lecturer ask questions and learn from each other.

It's no surprise CU's events are widely attended and receive raving reviews. Participants are invited to actively participate, and what they contribute affects the event's flow. This is the surest way to make sure participants can receive meaningful takeaways from the experience.

* * *

How to Make Any Experience Transformational

When we think of transformative events, our minds automatically revert to the "special" ones—conferences, celebrations, and performances that require months of preparation. It's important to recognize *any* interaction has the potential to transform a community member in some fundamental way. If transformation was reserved exclusively for one-in-a-blue-moon events, it would be impossible for members to realize their full potential.

So, what makes tiny, everyday moments powerful?

Think back to the moments where you reflected, "Wow, I never thought about it that way before" or "I wish I could stay in this moment forever." What was the specific action that catalyzed it? For example, here are some truly transformational moments I experienced within digital communities:

- The first time someone told me they loved me (platonically, as a friend) over Slack. I'd never had someone say that outside of my family before. Growing up, love was often tied to achievement, and I developed an irrational fear I was unlovable. This experience helped me reframe that mental model, externalize my misconception, and realize how much that person and community meant to me.

- Laughing so hard on a Zoom call I doubled over in my seat and turned my video off. We had been working non-stop for weeks on an important project, were honestly bone-tired, and probably laughing over something insignificant. That day, I saw a side to community members I didn't know existed... It reminded me of 3 a.m. hotel parties at FBLA conferences where people are 1) super tired, 2) hustling like crazy because the competition is the next day, and 3) bonding over the sheer absurdity of the situation.

- A really good jam with two close friends over Zoom. It happened after a raw week in the community, and the jam itself felt like an unveiling. We shared our experiences (more similar than I expected), acknowledged each other's work, talked through next steps, laughed, cried, and came to new realizations about the community and my role in it. When previous to the conversation I felt like my world was falling apart, I left feeling grounded and grateful.

You can weave the same type of transformation I experienced into the fabric of your community's experiences. It seems like these moments are all over the place, but they share common threads. Some of these threads include:

- **Create first, best, and unusual experiences**. By definition, these experiences have the potential for transformation! Try to mix up the events in your community, introduce fun and spontaneity, and challenge members to try new things. From a Zoom yoga session (if that's not a practice your community usually engages in) to encouraging members to facilitate a dialogue, experiment with new community opportunities. Encourage members to organize these as well, because they know what they want best!

- **Spotlight transformation that has already occurred.** Transformational experiences happen to us all the time; we simply find it challenging to pinpoint them because we're not trained to reflect on these moments. It feels like we experience "gradual growth," when in reality, growth is distributed unevenly over time. We experience great growth during small moments of chaos and amazement (think eureka moments). A big part of helping people experience transformation is helping them notice what has already happened. This isn't the same as forcing or implying transformation, which can feel performative and uncomfortable. Rather, you're allowing people to share if they have experienced it. You can model this practice by sharing *your* own transformation, using phrases like...
  - "This conversation is so good because..."
  - "What you just said is making me realize..."
  - "One of the biggest things I'm taking away from this conversation is..."
- **Uplift people's contributions.** Emphasizing how much someone has added to a conversation and helping them feel as if they are *making history* is powerful. Not only does it feel great, it prompts that person and those around them to notice the contribution, see it in a new light, and make new meaning from it. Uplifting contributions is as simple as saying "thank you for sharing that" or "well said." These affirmations help community members feel like they're helping others have transformative experiences, which is transformational in itself!

- **Create something together.** Nothing is more transformational than actualizing an idea over the course of a conversation or event. When possible, shift focus from just talking to creating something together, whether it's prototyping a new event series or engaging in a gratitude practice. Remember your "creation" doesn't need to be extravagant. It can be as simple as writing down key insights during a brainstorming session, or documenting learning another way.

* * *

Learning Together

In addition to events and everyday moments, a couple specific experiences foster and accelerate transformation. One of these is learning together.

It's no surprise new information prompts us to evolve our mental models and corresponding actions. For example, I learned so much about what it means to nurture deep connections and find meaning in everyday events through Casper ter Kuile's *The Power of Ritual*. I started becoming aware of society's dominant paradigm of the world: the story of more. In the story of more, productivity is one-dimensional, and growth means producing. We are expected to chase the next goal, move fast and break things along the way.

Through the book, I learned about a different form of growth, one built on slowing down and cultivating trust. I learned to see goals as milestones in a values-driven life, not something to be put on a pedestal. I started going on walks in the middle of the day. I started playing piano after dinner. I started having sleepovers with my sisters, growing a plant, and even taking periodic tech sabbaths—twenty-four hours of not using my laptop or phone.

Powerful, right? I changed my entire life, from a single book!

Here's the secret: I didn't do it alone.

Even though I wasn't in a Power of Ritual book club and no friends or family participated in tech sabbaths with me, I was lucky to be part of communities in which I could share my learnings with others. I was having conversations with people about leading with love, creating restorative spaces, and imagining civic religion. I told all my friends I was doing tech sabbaths (even updating my status in certain Slack workspaces), and fellow community members asked how it was going. All of this transformation happened for me with lots of individual learning and some light support from community.

Just imagine what is possible when community members learn together from the very beginning and apply learnings collectively. Instead of feeling crazy about taking a tech sabbath, I'd have a tribe of people doing the same thing. We can hold each other accountable, share best practices, test ideas and assumptions... Transformation will come easier and also feel more complete.

Normally, it's quite hard to find a group of people willing to experiment with you (my sisters definitely thought I went crazy when I started tech sabbaths). Luckily, you've already found your tribe! The people in your community probably have similar passions and seek to learn similar things. Now, it's simply a matter of how to structure your learning for maximum impact—which is where cohorts and STEVEs come in.

Cohort-based STEVEs

Few of us have glowing impressions of online learning. For me, I think of virtual school (no thanks) and massive open online courses (MOOCs), like EdX or Coursera. Productivity and online education expert Tiago Forte calls MOOCs the first wave of online learning, which involves traditional educational institutions putting lectures online. MOOCs democratize access to a wide variety of content and make learning affordable and accessible. Learners can register for courses, move at their own pace, and emerge with new knowledge and practical skills.

It sounds awesome. Even still, I have never successfully completed a MOOC. And it's not just me—few people who start MOOCs actually complete them. Justin Reich and José Ruipérez-Valiente from MIT's Teaching Systems Lab report in the journal *Science* that among all participants enrolled in MIT and Harvard's EdX courses in 2017-2018, only 3.13 percent completed them.

Without a *community* of folks learning with and supporting MOOC participants, it's hard to find motivation to push through. When it comes to MOOCs, optionality does not imply quality, much less accountability. Signing up says very little about whether you will complete it or put into practice what you learned, which real transformation requires.

Tiago Forte offers two frameworks to design online learning experiences that produce a transformational impact on learners: STEVEs and cohort-based courses.

STEVEs, which stands for "short, tiny, exclusive virtual experiences," describe the second wave of online education. STEVEs still leverage digital technologies to create the accessibility of MOOCs, but are designed to foster accountability by allowing individuals to learn with a distributed peer group.

STEVEs are designed to be...

- **Short.** Set learning goals that are time bound. STEVEs that go on forever lead to procrastination and unfinished work.
- **Tiny.** Cultivate personal interactions in small group settings. Learners are motivated and held accountable by fellow learners they know and don't want to let down.
- **Exclusive.** Create barriers of entry to join the STEVE. People love being part of limited-enrollment, invite-only, selective experiences.
- **Virtual.** Deliver content online. The many community technologies described in Chapter 2.3: Technology allow people to make learning more real and interconnected.
- **Experiences.** Fun, intense, skills-based, and challenging experiences serve as a "pressure cooker" for friendships to form and deepen.

More recently, Forte describes the idea of cohort-based courses: groups of learners who join an online course together and move through at the same pace. The course instructor offers valuable guidance to help learners master the material, but learning happens peer-to-peer instead of top down. Courses become something learners participate in beyond just content consumption.

Communities have always known what cohorts have just discovered: bringing together a group of people over and over again, over a topic everyone cares about, is powerful. The learning community that emerges enables...

- **True accountability**—high challenge and high support is possible when people are in healthy relationships.
- **Joyful interaction**—people are invited to step outside their comfort zones and bring more aspects of their humanity into their learning: vulnerable sharing, laughing and crying, changing their mind, and expressing their authentic selves.
- **High impact**—content is delivered with love and rigor, which infuses meaning and transforms someone so thoroughly they barely recognize themselves on the other side (a good thing)!

It's clear how STEVEs are best run in small cohorts. At the end of the day, it's about both learning and community building. When trust and camaraderie are present, people can better support each other's exploration, share discoveries, and make sense of the world together. Community members naturally want to share their unique insights. When they do, it starts a positive feedback cycle of people surfacing new knowledge and applying it to the real world.

* * *

Rituals

Another type of experience that engenders transformation are rituals: recurring actions designed to strengthen a sense of belonging in a community. In contrast to events or cohort-based STEVEs, rituals are symbolic experiences that help members find meaning through the community.

Surprisingly, most rituals are casual, everyday things. Growing up, I felt anchored at home because of the rituals my dad created, from weekly Saturday family movie nights and Sunday mahjong to celebrating every birthday with a chocolate ice cream cake.

In addition to the everyday rituals, there's a particular type of ritual that is more majestic in volume and stance. These rituals, called rites of passages, are repeated less frequently but on a larger scale by an entire community. Rites of passages, often more ceremonial and coordinated, mark major experiences or milestones in someone's life, such as the quinceañera and sweet sixteen, or senior prom and graduation. In doing so, they formalize someone's transformation into a new stage of life.

Casper ter Kuile, author of *The Power of Ritual*, describes how rituals are the "patterned, repeated ways in which we enact the moral emotions—compassion, gratitude, awe, bliss, empathy, ecstasy," and how doing so allows us to create patterns of the greatest capacities, such as the "capacity to share, to sing, to chant, to revere, to find beauty, to dance, to imagine, to quietly reflect, to sense something beyond what we see." When we embed ritual into the fabric of our communities, we not only do more of what feels joyful and meaningful, we notice the people around us and move into a community mindset.

Rituals are actions done with intention, attention, and repetition, that infuse tradition into your community. They strengthen bonds between members and embody the community's values. Being part of rituals helps members feel like they are part of a larger whole.

In her book *Braving the Wilderness*, Brené Brown describes the concept of collective effervescence: an experience of connection, communal emotion, and a "sensation of sacredness" that happens when we are part of something bigger than ourselves. People who frequently feel this way experience significance and worth. Their lives become coherent and driven by purpose. Rituals are one of the most powerful ways to create collective effervescence, which leads to self-transcendence and transformation. So, how might we create rituals?

What are rituals?

Contrary to popular belief, rituals don't have to be extravagant. There's a popular misconception that rituals are only for religious people or those who are part of a cult—which is not true at all!

In fact, in *The Power of Ritual*, ter Kuile talks about how we can turn everyday practices—like yoga, reading, and walking the dog—into sacred rituals that allow us to deeply connect with others and transform ourselves. What makes something a ritual isn't necessarily *what* you do together, but *how* you do it. It rests on members to infuse rituals with meaning.

For example, imagine two groups doing the same exercise: meditation. Group A sits together for five minutes and are told to meditate. Members frown impatiently, tap their feet, check their phones, and half-heartedly close their eyes for a few seconds and call it meditation. This group probably didn't get much from the event, given members were distracted and unfocused. They weren't present together. It was a waste of time and created frustration.

In contrast, members in Group B sit in a circle to meditate. A facilitator sets intentions at the beginning of their practice, and invites members to slow down, sink into silence, and listen to their intuition. People realize meditating together is even more powerful than meditating alone. The group commits to executing this practice every morning for the next month. It's much more likely along the way, Group B arrives at new realizations about themselves and the world around them.

The differences between Groups A and B, between what is meaningful and what isn't, between what can be called a ritual and what can't, are three things:

- **Intention**—what thoughts, feelings, and energies are you inviting into this moment?
- **Attention**—do you come back to the present moment, even when your attention starts to drift? Noticing your body, fellow community members, and living beings around you leads to greater intention.
- **Repetition**—how many times has this practice been done? Of course, not everything should be repeated, but when the right practice comes along, repetition accrues meaning.

Designing rituals

You can think about ritual creation in two phases: discovery and design.

First, it's important to discover moments in your community with the capacity to hold meaning and symbolism. These actions should also be easily repeated and accessible to your members. You might think about things your community already does together. Maybe you start off every event with an icebreaker question or piece of poetry. Maybe you close every meeting with a reflection question like "What is something you think everyone should do at least once in their lives?" and wave goodbye after people share their answer. Maybe your community coordinates birthday videos for your most active members.

After you decide on an action, the next step is to design an experience that adds greater meaning and depth. In a Ritual Design Lab article, Kursat Ozenc explains rituals mark an event where "the ordinary is suspended for a certain time, and a magic moment occurs." This magic moment comes from helping people craft a new story about who they are and the values they hold (their aspirational selves), then allowing them to embody that new story during the ritual. Rituals provide a specific instance where people participate in behavior.

For example, I have rituals that prepare me for my tech sabbath: physically cleaning my desk, writing down ten things I'm grateful for, doing five minutes of guided meditation, then watching my laptop power down. As I do this, I'm redefining a part of my life narrative, telling the story that I'm the type of person who slows down, evokes a calming presence, and emanates quiet joy.

Ozenc has identified five elements successful rituals use to create new narrative arcs. Reflect on where each of these components show up in your ritual design:

- **Trigger**. What in your schedule or the natural world triggers the ritual? It can be a certain day of the week, whenever it starts raining, a team member's birthday, or something else entirely.

- **Intention spell.** What is the purpose of your ritual? What are the values or aspirational selves the ritual brings forth? Without intention, ritual is a mindless routine.
- **Script.** What is the beginning, middle, and end to your ritual? A ritual flow contributes to a sense of coherence.
- **Props.** Is there a symbolic object the ritual is centered around? It can be anything from sharing food to wearing costumes to listening to a certain type of music.
- **Enactment.** What energy do people bring to the ritual? Having a plan for how rituals unfold is great, but it's up to participants to take on and identify with the new narrative.

Finally, as you think about the components of the narrative arc, don't forget rituals require intention and attention *over time*. Don't skimp on the reps!

Community experiences, designed and executed correctly, create evangelists of your community. When members feel like they are constantly levelling up into better versions of themselves, they are more likely to stick around and leave a positive mark on your community!

2.6

ESTABLISH YOUR VIBE

———

"Once you truly understand that you are just beautiful energy wrapped in human form, your fear and 'otherness' will disappear and you will experience deep belonging and fellowship."

—RADHA AGRAWAL

If you've ever met someone and didn't hang out with them because they had "bad vibes," you're not alone. As a kid, I was incredibly critical of people with bad vibes, refusing to hang out with them at recess. My mom would tell me not to "judge people so quickly," assuming my perception was a mere subjective preference. But what if it was more than that?

Bad vibes signal someone is out of touch with their values, strengths, passions, or long-term goals. They are distracted. Their priorities are distorted. It's hard for someone with no consistency in their actions to live a life of increasing integrity, virtue, and meaning. Your intuition is telling you to avoid misalignment, and more often than not, it's the right decision. By disengaging people with bad vibes, we protect our ability to stay on an upward trajectory.

An important disclaimer: Bad vibes should not be treated as an absolute, especially when meeting someone for the first time. While we often form first impressions of people based on impermanent factors, like what they are wearing, their mood, how they greet you, and what they're doing in the moment, these are all fleeting factors. However, there's a persistent set of beliefs that underlies a person's vibe. When thinking about capturing your vibe, consider both the surface-level aesthetics and deeper stories—because over time, members will notice if your community's core beliefs don't align with external signals!

Just like people, communities have vibes too. And just like we avoid people with bad vibes, we tend to also avoid communities with bad vibes... While vibes seem invisible, unquantifiable, and mysterious, that doesn't negate their importance.

What counts as a "good vibe" and what are they composed of?

In an essay for *The New Yorker*, author Kyle Chayka writes, "What a haiku is to language, a vibe is to sensory perception: a concise assemblage of image, sound, and movement. A vibe can be positive, negative, beautiful, ugly, or just unique. It can even become a quality in itself: if something is vibey, it gives off an intense vibe or is particularly amenable to vibes. Vibes are a medium for feeling, the kind of abstract understanding that comes before words put a name to experience. That pre-linguistic quality makes them well suited to a social-media landscape that is increasingly prioritizing audio, video, and images over text. Through our screens, vibes are being constantly emitted and received."

Let's break that down. Chayka outlines...

- Vibe describes how we perceive a space.
- The vibe is an intangible but distinct feeling, almost like a magical aura.
- Both good and bad vibes exist. A community with a good vibe might be exciting/healing/enlightening/inspiring. One with a bad vibe, or no vibe, might be dull/tedious/tiring/draining.
- A community that does not have the right vibe lacks certain elements of *life* (image, sound, movement). The elements present do not evoke the positive feelings members are expecting.

A more familiar word for vibe might be **energy**. In her book *Belong*, Radha Agrawal, co-founder, CEO, and chief community architect of Daybreaker, describes how community architecture is essentially thoughtful energy curation. "Energy defines how we feel and how others perceive us more than any other quality," Agrawal writes. "Energy is a great equalizer in life. It doesn't matter what you do for a living or how much money you have—the energy you put out is the energy you get back. Negative energy breeds negative community. Positive energy breeds positive community. It's that simple."

And it's true. A few things happen once organic exchanges between community members start to produce trust, reciprocity, and good vibes.

First, the community's positive energy pours out and manifests as creative expression: memes, witty comments, internal language, and other artifacts that can only be created by members. Over time, communities externalize their artifacts, creating art, podcasts, newsletters, and whitepapers to share in public. When outsiders see how cool these artifacts are (it might have gained media and cultural attention), it creates FOMO. People want in on good vibes. Energy is infectious.

If you've followed the steps in this book, you have a solid foundation for your community. It's time to create and communicate the good vibes that make your community special and attract the best members. While a vibe can seem intangible, the practices that help you cultivate and express a good vibe are not. These things include your community's...

- **Beliefs** // Create your vibe. The beliefs community leaders and members hold and embody hugely impact their energy.
- **Artifacts and aesthetics** // Capture your vibe. Memes, hot takes, language, and branding all breathe life into your community.
- **Stories** // Share your vibe. Stories are how we make sense of our experiences. Our lives are devoted to telling stories about what we did, where we were, and who we were with.

* * *

Beliefs

Regardless of why your community exists or who it's created for, there are a set of vibes almost everyone wants to embody. People want to be part of exciting, healing, inspiring, and empowering things. As you might guess, these vibes do not magically appear.

Instead, what creates these "universally good vibes" are your community's mental models—thought processes about how something works in the real world. These thought processes create cascading effects on how you treat your members, how people show up, the energy they bring, and the resulting vibe.

For example, the *Harvard Business Review* discusses Theory X and Theory Y, two mental models around human motivation at work introduced by Douglas McGregor in the 1960s. Theory X sees employees as lazy, fear-motivated, and in need of constant direction, whereas Theory Y believes people are motivated by the value of their contribution.

Imagine you are a Theory X manager. Because people are lazy and fear-motivated, you institute strict work hours and hourly production targets. Every infraction leads to a deduction from the employee's monthly paycheck. This causes workers to show up just for the paycheck and drag their feet in case production targets get increased. The workplace brims with wariness and strife... not exactly the best vibe.

Now, you're a Theory Y manager. You believe people are reasonable and can be trusted to do the right thing. Trust is something lost, not gained. As a result, you remove production targets and the paycheck-deduction system based on clocked hours. You give employees the freedom to make decisions and experiment with ideas. People feel more responsibility for their work and take pride in a job well done. Instead of discontent, the workplace hums with spirit and ownership.

The differences between these mental models are significant.

What many people don't realize is these types of mental models also exist in our communities. Maybe not Theory X and Theory Y specifically, but we carry assumptions around how events should be run, how members relate to each other, and what we should spend our time doing. It's important to constantly interrogate and evolve our mental models to identify whether they are serving or harming our members. Individual mental models, especially those held by a community's primary stewards, have a huge effect on vibe.

To that end, here are four powerful mental model shifts that lead to universal good vibes:

Mandatory → opt-in

When possible, make events opt-in and let people choose whether they want to get involved! If you don't have great attendance, it's a sign people are not attaining value. Consider doing some community research (ask members what events they want to see) and iterate on the event format.

Opt-in is key because even just one person who doesn't want to be there can ruin the vibe for everyone else. We easily take on the energies of people around us!

The time young people are willing and able to commit ebbs and flows throughout the course of the year. For example, people might need to step back during finals week at school. Making a meeting mandatory then would be a disaster—people would be stressed, not focused (potentially multitasking and studying), maybe even resentful of the community for being intrusive and disrespecting important commitments. It's a recipe for creating the disastrous Group A meditation experience from the last chapter. Furthermore, you're fooling yourself if you make things "mandatory" in digital-first communities, because unlike work or school, no one has to be there anyway!

Allowing people to opt-in is how we can make every community event **exciting** for community members.

Comparison → Inspiration

"Competitive vibes" create toxic spaces that perpetuate a zero-sum, winner-takes-all narrative. When community members incessantly compare what they do or do not have, it leads to jealousy, resentment, and sabotage. What's ironic is as individuals try to be "better" than each other, the community as a whole engages in a race to the bottom where values are compromised and actions become increasingly questionable. Everyone becomes worse off.

Instead of comparing yourself to others, let differences serve as inspirations! When we do, we start to notice wonderful things about fellow members and appreciate them more. We're able to observe how those around us live their values and cultivate their gifts—and gain new ideas and motivation to do so ourselves. We start to appreciate the ways in which others have shaped our journeys. The entire community is placed on an upward trajectory where people constantly discover new inspirations and are acknowledged for being an inspiration to others.

In that process, members start to think about how their presence could be the spark that fuels someone else's upward trajectory. They recognize their power to start a chain reaction of "good vibes" that circulate around the community.

Ultimately, encouraging community members to see each other as **inspirations** helps us create a culture of gratitude and growth.

Scarcity →Abundance

Comparison is the root of another belief that doesn't serve our communities: the scarcity mindset.

The scarcity mindset tells us we are fundamentally separate individuals, and we need to compete with others to get what we need. In this mental model, no real safety exists in community. For example, someone might be unwilling to share scholarship opportunities with fellow community members because there are only a couple of scholarship recipients, and they feel a need to fight for those limited spots.

Instead, we need to create practices that help people see there is more than enough support and resources to go around. The abundance mindset is about creating more of what we need, which is easily achieved in community. With the scholarship scenario, an abundance mindset recognizes circulating opportunities is a good thing. When one person starts sharing resources, others will do so as well. And when someone from the community wins the scholarship, the scholarship recipient will discover new networks and new opportunities to share.

The abundance mindset won't happen automatically. It requires a tremendous amount of trust, transparency, and communication. But with the structures and processes introduced in earlier chapters, abundance becomes increasingly possible. When your community replaces scarcity with abundance, members are able to practice more...

- **Generosity**—sharing time, knowledge, and energy with others. Generous support is less about transactional trading or bartering, and more about recirculating resources and gently meeting needs. When we're individually trying to maximize our slice of the pie, we don't notice just how big the pie can be if we put our slices together. Generosity helps people discover the safety and security they are chasing.

- **Self-care**—especially if you're part of an impact-focused community, it can feel like there's a never-ending list of things to advocate for. It's important to remind members they are not alone. There's a whole community of people who can and want to support them! At every moment, contribution to the collective should energize members. Encouraging people to recharge increases their capacity to opt-in over time and bring their best energy into the work.

Inviting people to make decisions from a place of abundance helps us create a **healing** space for community members.

Talking → Taking Action

People need to be doing things to be healthy. There are always things to work on, grow toward, get better at, and learn about in order to become more like our aspirational selves. When members are in the doing mode, they are able to make tangible contributions toward a better world.

Whereas talking is stationary, doing is generative. Generative energy is critical in communities, which require constant growth and transformative experiences to flourish.

At the end of the day, no one wants to just sit around talking about their vision for the future. We're often stuck in spaces that value eloquence, where your actions are not as important as your ability to string together the right buzzwords to sound important. I can say from firsthand experience it's draining and discouraging to be surrounded by people too busy fretting about looking good they forget there's an entire component called doing good.

Digital-first communities are one of the rare places where young people have a *real* opportunity to create change with the support of those around them. The things that weren't possible for an individual to accomplish suddenly become feasible when a group decides to pool their resources and work together to turn ideas into reality.

Help community members experience what it feels like to have agency over the future. Instead of building your community *for* your people, build it *with* them. Trust members to have good ideas and know what they need—and let them experiment! Draw upon the abundance mindset and help people realize they have power (knowledge, support, resources) to take action now.

Focusing the community's energy on taking action instead of talking **empowers** community members to realize their visions for the future.

* * *

Aesthetics and artifacts

When we think of vibe, the first things that come to mind are often surface level aesthetics: your logo, colors, and fonts. Kyle Chayka explains in *The New Yorker*, "#Aesthetic is sometimes used to mark vibes, but that term is predominantly visual." Essentially, aesthetics are the visual representation of your community's energy!

Even if it seems shallow, how your community presents itself matters. Just think of how many times we pull away from something because it's not "aesthetically pleasing." Unappealing aesthetics make a community less accessible. For example, imagine a middle school STEM club with recruitment posters that are dark blue and feature images of LEGOs, race cars, and male action figures. Intentionally or not, the poster plays into stereotypes and alienates those who don't find the symbols aesthetically pleasing. Instead, space or nature might be a more neutral aesthetic that still aligns with the STEM mission.

Beyond capturing the look and feel of your community, aesthetics serve to build camaraderie and create familiarity between members. Pieces of your community's aesthetic should work together to make someone *feel* a certain way and inspire the vibe your community wants to create.

Aesthetics are one of the most underappreciated aspects of community architecture. It's a simple way to capture your vibe and share it with the world, as well as helping attract the right members. But it also requires a certain degree of style and cultural awareness from the aesthetic designer; without it, there are many ways for a community's aesthetic to flop or appear out of touch.

The good news is you don't have to tackle aesthetics alone! Being the community builder doesn't mean you're also the aesthetic designer. In fact, aesthetics can naturally emerge from community members. You might notice people using certain fonts, colors, or metaphors to describe the community and their role in it. Anything created by members, from memes to event flyers to end-of-the-year celebration videos, contributes to the aesthetic. Identifying patterns between artifacts can help you capture your vibe and home in on your community's messaging.

Finally, remember your community's aesthetic can and will change over time. Just like how rules, events, and other components of your community respond to members' ever-shifting wants and needs, aesthetics do so as well. Aesthetic creation isn't a forced process, but rather one that emerges organically from members.

Artifacts that Capture Your Aesthetic

As you think about how to capture your community's vibe, here are a couple types of tangible products that package your aesthetic to share with the outside world.

Pay attention to instances where members take initiative to create some of these things (most frequently with language and memes). Find ways to uplift their efforts. Aesthetics are most authentic when they emerge from the energy and imagination of members themselves. That said, don't be afraid to ask for volunteers either and nudge people to help create certain artifacts, especially if it will create personal growth opportunities for them.

Here are four broad categories of artifacts to consider:

- **Branding**. This includes everything you normally think of when figuring how to package and market a product (in this case, a community). It's everything that captures your look and feel, including name, slogan, logo, color palette, and font guide. Branding is one of the first things prospective members see and interact with, so it's critical it not only reflects your community's vibe, but something about it stands out.

- To put into perspective how much branding matters, imagine a member onboarding handbook written in Comic Sans with pieces of text highlighted in bright colors and funny gifs breaking up the text. Now, imagine the same document but in Times New Roman, and instead of highlights, certain headings are bolded with passages italicized. Very different vibes, right?
- When it comes to branding, it's important to think ahead. Ideally, people will be able to easily recognize and rally around your brand, and the brand can be remixed to meet the evolving needs of members. Consider questions like: How will my logo look placed on swag items? Is our name too many syllables or hard to pronounce? Does our color palette interact well with the metaphors we use to describe our community?

- **Language.** What your members call themselves and how they speak with each other matters. Words define what is important and establish a conceptual framework through which members make sense of the community. Language is how we use those words to convey energy. Words and shared language enable people to relate and orient themselves to the community and each other.

  - Often, words in the English language don't fully capture what we want to express. In that case, encourage your community to coin terms that work for you! Having words and language unique to your community is a simple way to increase belonging. For example, Civics Unplugged popularized terms like *unplugging* from extracurriculars and mental models that aren't serving you, in order to *plug into* things that help you realize your full potential. In the CU community, young people are called *Builders* and *civic superheroes* because we all have unique superpowers we use to help build the future of humanity. Before we had these terms, a civic-minded young person would have been chalked up to an "activist," which can have very limiting and even negative connotations.

- And it's not just words—diction and tone are core aspects of someone's language. For example, is it okay to curse in your community? Do facilitators sound urgent or peaceful during a Zoom call? How loud do people usually talk?

- Finally, things like emojis, the number of exclamation marks people use, and whether messages are written in lower or upper case also subtly shapes interaction between members. Intentionally or not, uppercase can have an aggressive vibe to it, especially since we don't usually text our friends with full sentences, punctuation, and capitalized letters!

- **Memes**. For most of my life, I thought memes were funny viral images. That was before I discovered **memetics**: a concept for how memes are self-replicating units of culture, and these contagious ideas, often captured in images, can do incredible good or bad. Eugene Wei, former Head of Product at Flipboard and Hulu, describes memes as "content with built-in distribution" (like TikTok dance #challenges) optimized for acquisition and transmission between human minds. Any thriving community wants a meme about itself to exist, which directs media and cultural attention to the community's vision.

  - If words and language are so important, remember the phrase "an image is worth a thousand words."

– Memes live on a rapid birth-death cycle, and the success of memes is often dependent upon the speed at which they spread within the public. The moment a meme stops spreading, it dies and disappears. This phenomenon is why enlisting members to create artifacts like memes is so important—decentralized meme-creation is the only way to keep up with the speed of meme culture.

– A good case study of memes in action is Bernie Sanders' 2020 presidential campaign. Bernie became the Democratic party's most meme-able candidate thanks to subreddit communities like r/SandersForPresident and r/OurPresident, which total over 564,000 users. Reddit is a website community and social platform where users can post links, comments, questions, and upvote or downvote posts to surface popular opinions. Partly due to its younger audience, Reddit largely prioritizes memes and serves as a huge marketplace for meme creation and dissemination, such as the "I am once again asking for your support" and the "Bernie or Hillary?" memes, which generated free publicity for Sanders' campaign. The energy behind these memes no doubt contributed to Bernie's rise in popularity among Gen Zers. Imagine if your community was able to tap into this power as well!

• **Other artifacts.** In addition to the ones shared above, so many other artifacts result from the creative energy of community members. These are everything from hot takes and inside jokes to music videos and community artwork. Artifacts can be circulated internally within the community to deepen culture and boost morale, or with the outside world to let them know what your community is all about (and create a sense of FOMO for prospective members).

– As a digital community and its aesthetic become more established, people from outside the community will notice and want in. It can be difficult to identify whether a certain artifact is intended to remain in the community to foster closeness, or if it's meant to be shared with the world. When in doubt, let members decide! It's important to ensure members are on board before you externalize your community's social products.

– Artifacts are most effective at capturing the vibe when they arise organically. Helping curate a community's aesthetics should be fun and freeing. The *process* of creating new artifacts should embody the vibes those artifacts portray!

Aesthetics manifest in many forms. What they all share is they're produced through playful exchanges of community members built on trust and good vibes.

In the beginning, the community builder often lays the minimum viable aesthetics, typically brand and language. As the community grows and members take ownership, they will start to shape branding and language to reflect their perceptions of the community. Frequent interactions between fellow members create the closeness and chemistry needed for memes and other artifacts to emerge.

Remember: A community's potential for creative production is unmeasurable. You have a bunch of committed people hyped to be in the same space and eager to *build* together—and energy is infectious. One of the smartest things a community builder can do is give capable community members free reign to capture vibe. Search for creative folks who love memes, always know the latest TikTok trends, and have great personal style. This might be their you-shaped hole!

Finally, capturing your vibe isn't a top-down process. Don't force the creation of aesthetics, especially if the energy isn't there or there isn't someone with the creative savvy to spearhead the process. It's better to have no memes than cringey ones. When it comes to aesthetics, quality always trumps quantity.

* * *

Stories

Storytelling makes up the bulk of our lives.

We tell stories for entertainment, but also because stories ground us. They help us find coherence and meaning in our experiences, make sense of the world, and deepen relationships with the people around us. Stories are often created about some experience, insight, or value discovered through community.

National Geographic explains how stories inform and propagate cultural values and traditions. "Not all of these stories are historically accurate or even true. Truth is less important than providing cultural cohesion," their website says. "[Stories] can encompass myths, legends, fables, religion, prayers, proverbs, and instructions." Stories help share information, including that of a community's vibe, in a memorable way.

If there aren't existing stories, outsiders and new community members will fill the gap with their own interpretations of the community's vibe. You'll end up with variations of why your community exists that might be unrepresentative of your brand, which creates confusion among members.

Imagine you want to communicate that your community has an introspective vibe, where members often engage in contemplative reflection *with* each other. You can do this in a couple ways:

1. Say the community is introspective, thoughtful, and collaborative.
2. Recite a list of things members do and use these isolated activities as evidence; we have a daily morning meditation practice, weekly character development groups, and a couple of our members even run an online yoga class for local middle school students.
3. Tell a story about how your community members came to adopt the practices above, why they matter, and how these practices have transformed members over time.

If you've heard "show, not tell" before, the same concept is applied here. We want to show people the vibe and help them reach the conclusion themselves. Simply telling them doesn't stick as long. Instead of relying on a list of vibes or stand-alone artifacts, storytelling enables you to package your community's vibe into shareable narratives that are enjoyable to listen to.

When crafting stories, we can draw on the work of Marshall Ganz, community organizer and senior lecturer in leadership, organizing, and civil society at Harvard University. Ganz describes a concept called "public narrative," which brings three stories into one: the story of self, the story of us, and the story of now.

- **Story of self**—a personal story that shows "why you were called to what you have been called to." The story of self is different for every community member, and helps listeners empathize with and relate to the storyteller.
- **Story of us**—a collective story that illustrates the "shared purposes, goals, and vision" of your community. It helps people understand who is gathering together and why, and invites them to be a part of it.
- **Story of now**—an urgent call to action that presents "the challenge this community faces, the choices it must make, and the hope to which 'we' can aspire." This story invites people to see themselves as part of the collective we and join you in taking action on the pressing challenge.

Because vibe is so dependent on the energies every member brings, invite each person to contribute a story of self that expresses their experience in a unique way. By helping members craft their own public narratives, your community can create a collection of stories that bring your vibe to life.

Ultimately, vibes are intangible markers of creative energy and culture that affect how people both in and out of your community perceive it. They are most clearly manifested through surface-level aesthetics and artifacts but informed by the deeper mental models and public narratives community members hold.

It's worthwhile to re-emphasize as the community builder, you are not forcing good vibes to emerge (it would be silly to tell everyone "Smile and be happy" at a party). Instead, create the right conditions that help members experience positive energy, tap into that energy through creative expression, and proudly share the creative artifacts with others.

How might we inspire folks to take initiative? Read on to find out!

2.7

EMPOWER NEW LEADERS

"Here we stumble upon a beautiful paradox: People can hold different levels of power, and yet everyone can be powerful... In an ecosystem, interconnected organisms thrive without one holding power over another. A fern or mushroom can express its full selfhood without ever reaching out as far into the sky as the tree next to which it grows. Through a complex collaboration involving exchanges of nutrients, moisture, and shade, the mushroom, fern, and tree don't compete but cooperate to grow into the biggest and healthiest versions of themselves."

—FREDERIC LALOUX

In the early stages of a community, it might feel like you are hustling 24/7 to build all the community infrastructure. You are the person who finds the people, chooses the tech platform, creates the space, and fills it with transformational experiences. Your initial investment of time and work is critical activation energy to get your community off the ground. That said, this energy is not sustainable.

As I interviewed community builders for this book, I heard from many people who described their community as "their baby" and themselves as "the mom" of the group. Folks spent so much time catering to and creating a perfectly smooth experience for members it felt right to use this metaphor.

Here's the problem: You're creating a community, not a family! Odds are people *don't* want you to be their mom and solve all their problems. As most teenagers have experienced before, we want the freedom to explore, to make mistakes and learn from them, and gain real influence by taking responsibility for our actions.

Shopify's CEO, Tobias Lütke, put it best. In an email to employees earlier this year, Lütke wrote, "Shopify, like any other for-profit company, is not a family. The very idea is preposterous. You are born into a family. You never choose it, and they can't un-family you... The dangers of 'family thinking' are that it becomes incredibly hard to let poor performers go. Shopify is a *team*, not a family." Throughout high school, I remember calling certain clubs a "second family"—a nice sentiment, but also one that nurtured unrealistic expectations. Family thinking can give people an unhealthy, overly dependent relationship with your community.

Furthermore, the power dynamics between mom (you) and kids (community members) are deeply asymmetrical and just plain weird. Kids depend on their parents for financial support, a roof over their heads, and food on the table. Not only do parents have direct legal power over their kids, they often have incredible emotional power over them as well... not necessarily the type of relationship you want to replicate in a flourishing community. So how do we unplug from the mom mindset and help our communities thrive? The answer is simple: Share power. At its core, community building is about building power in people. Instead of mom being the "glue" that holds the family together, it's about members bonding through their own interactions and shared experiences. It's about building *with* others. It's about baking empowerment into the structure and practices of your community, so people can make their own connections, reach out for new opportunities, and take on leadership.

Furthermore, the mom mindset isn't even helpful for us. It leads to micromanagement and increased stress on the community builder, while decreasing meaningful collaboration with members.

Like how taking care of kids is a huge commitment in both time and energy, the same can be said for community building. Time is something young people, who spend a significant portion of their lives at school and juggle many commitments, often do not have. As a result, it inhibits our ability to flourish when we try to shoulder the process of community building by ourselves.

I have met far too many community builders staying up until 2 a.m. throwing together a run of show for their community's next event, all the while feeling resentful and drained. What's ironic is community builders want to create the opposite vibe for members. But how can you create something for others you aren't experiencing yourself? And if you're creating the event from a place of burn-out, how can you expect that to not affect the event's design and execution?

Sharing power not only creates new leaders, which is essential to your community's longevity, it's also a practice of self-preservation. A community isn't a community until it's organizing itself.

So how might we empower new leaders who can dedicate their time and energy to the community?

Most people can get behind the first strategy: Empowering new leaders is a process that starts with the current leaders becoming more aware. Current leaders can become better listeners, learn to step back, lift up marginalized voices, and acknowledge others' contributions.

There's certainly room for a more conscious and caring brand of leadership. But what people don't realize is sharing power is about more than that.

The narrative above assumes all the power is centralized with a small number of leaders at the top of the hierarchy. That elite group of leaders need to be thoughtful and benevolent enough to share their power with everyone else, who have none! In this model, only a small number of people can be new leaders... There's only so much power to go around.

This is where the second strategy comes in: Empowerment isn't just given; it must be baked into the structures and practices of your community. Instead of something fought over, power becomes something people simply *have*. It's no longer zero-sum, where more power for me means less for you. Instead, power can be created, because every member has the support and resources they need to spark change in their corner of the community. When one of us becomes more powerful, all of us become more powerful as well. Gaining power means increasing your capacity to support other's efforts in even more effective ways.

Suddenly, everyone can become a new leader—a realization that is increasingly valuable as your community scales. Returning to our garden metaphor, instead of a select few "leaders" tending the garden and getting burnt out because there's so much to do, everyday garden visitors have the power to trim a leaf here and pull out a weed there. Power comes from a combination of the core garden tenders inviting visitor insights around how the community can improve, as well as making resources needed to take action available to visitors, like a list of weeds and gardening shears. Having many people organically notice problems and step up to tend them makes your garden more resilient in the long run.

Here are the two strategies we discuss in this chapter:

1. **Lead with love** // Help people want to lead. This is the more conscious and caring brand of leadership. While leading with love isn't everything, it helps people feel valued and needed, two key characteristics of people inspired to contribute to the community in bigger ways.

2. **Decentralize power** // Make it easy for people to lead. This is the empowerment baked into your community's structure and practices, so people *already have power* and don't need to wait for existing leaders to give it to them. It's about creating wells of resources and support anyone can draw on to make their corner of the community better.

* * *

Leading with Love

Love is constantly expanding your sense of self. It's realizing how interconnected we all are (when you're more powerful, I am more powerful), and helping each other show up as the best versions of ourselves. Doing so engenders true liberation, which priest and author Henri Nouwen describes as "freeing people from the bonds that have prevented them from giving their gifts to others."

When people are led lovingly, they feel...

- Seen and heard
- Freed to express themselves authentically and vulnerably
- Validated and appreciated for their ideas and emotions
- Capable of making tangible contributions that push the community forward
- **Valued and needed** for the community's collective flourishing

Love helps people feel affirmed in who they are, recognized for their superpowers, and valued for their contributions—all without the need for a "title" in the community. It helps people see how the community wouldn't be the same without their energy, imagination, and leadership. It helps people notice all the strengths they bring to the table, whether that's strategic vision, project management experience, or simply a calming presence.

The moment people start to feel truly liberated is the moment they become a leader in your community. So, what does liberating love look and feel like? Inclusion and trust.

Inclusion

Inclusion creates a persistent sense that our efforts are seen and that we have people rooting for us, which gives us confidence and security to step up and lead, even if we might fail. Historically, conversations around inclusion have centered on identity. How do we design spaces for the most marginalized among us? As we discussed in Chapter 2.2: Finding Your People, we need to be increasingly intentional about who is in and who is out—and how we prioritize the people meant to be in through thoughtful barriers to entry. Often, exclusion for some means inclusion for others.

For example, at Ethel's Club, a NY-based membership club made by and for people of color, the people meant to be "in" are prioritized at every touchpoint. According to founder Naj Austin, everything from the art and plants to the electricians and contractors were "influenced, created, or sourced by someone who believes in the same credo—for us, by us." When people experience a space designed for them, when they realize *they themselves* have a deep understanding of what fellow community members need, and when they see people who look like them already leading, stepping into leadership becomes much more feasible.

There are also many other dimensions of inclusion outside of identity.

Inclusion can mean building ways for people with different strengths to contribute, or people with variable time commitments to stay in the loop. Members come with all sorts of lived experiences and everyday realities beyond their roles in the community. In order to ensure everyone is included and has an equal opportunity to lead, it's critical to build in optionality. Some strategies to do this include...

- **Normalize rest.** Community members (and community builders!) cannot work all the time, nor should they be expected to. Few people want to step up to lead a community where they're expected to work non-stop or are asked to sacrifice their individual well-being, even if it's in the service of "doing good."
- **Make it easy to catch up.** Engagement ebbs and flows, especially in youth-centered communities. If someone needs to step back for a month during AP exams, make it easy for them to 1) figure out what went on while they were gone and 2) find ways to plug in when they return. The "catch up" process doesn't have to be explicit, which can make people feel shamed or falling behind. It can be embedded into weekly community calls, spontaneous jams with core members, a newsletter, or something else entirely.
- **Respect different levels of engagement.** It's critical to acknowledge contributions and leadership at all scales. Yes, be sure to recognize your most engaged and committed members—but don't exclusively shout out people who are able to dedicate ten or more hours. Not everyone can do that, and it alienates folks who might want to contribute but simply have less bandwidth. You're likely working closely with your biggest "hand raisers" anyway, so recognize them through other recurring interactions like small group team meetings or one-on-one syncs. Reserve a chunk of public appreciation for budding leaders and members who've contributed in small but mighty ways.

Trust

In *Untamed*, Glennon Doyle explains how liberating love requires trust.

There's a suffocating brand of love built around control, where we want the best for someone and decide the best way to achieve it is to take over their lives and make sure everything goes as planned. Sometimes, mom love falls into this category. But it's important to note: managing community members is not love.

Imagine how tiring it is to love someone and yet doubt every decision they make, distrust their judgment, and constantly shield them from the world. You wouldn't be able to engage in meaningful dialogue because you believe they aren't capable of grappling with reality. Healthy relationships would struggle to emerge from this dynamic, much less healthy communities.

Instead, we trust people we love.

Trust needs to exist for members to have courage to call out bad ideas, introduce new ones, and guide the community forward. Some strategies to create trust include...

- **Public reflection and appropriate responses.** Encouraging authentic, vulnerable reflection in your community is a subtle signal to members you trust them to hold space for what others share. With this trust comes a degree of personal responsibility and a request for everyday members to help steward the community. But it's not *just* about members' reflections—it's also how you, the community builder, respond to them. Reflections are a great opportunity for members to share disagreements, new ideas, and ways they desire to step up. Acknowledging and responding appropriately is essential to build trust, not just signal it.

- **Open agendas and dialogue.** Creating space for free-flowing dialogue shows you trust members to contribute important insights and help craft meaningful experiences, not just consume them. Create simple guardrails for events instead of a packed agenda to allow for more spontaneity. Trusting in the process and community members is not only liberating for all involved, but often yields beautiful results too!

- **Giving people responsibility.** It might seem obvious: If you want to show someone you trust them to do something, let them do it! That said, giving people responsibility does not mean throwing them in the deep end. If a community member has never hosted a group gathering before, you probably don't want them leading the next big event. Instead, gradually challenge people with new tasks and provide ample guidance and resources along the way. For example, members might…

  - Offer ideas and feedback—One of the simplest ways to loop members in is to ask them for their thoughts. This process is most effective when you approach them with a document, question, or other provocation.

  - Support facilitators behind the scenes—Running an event is no easy thing, and facilitators love any support they can get. Folks can volunteer to take notes, share screen, moderate chat, or another helpful role. This is a great way for members to step up, feel less out of place if new, and continue to learn about the community.

  - Lead or co-lead community events—This works especially well for events with highly documented processes. For example, Civics Unplugged's juntos (small discussion and mutual support groups) use the same agenda structure each week, which makes it easy for anyone to facilitate.

– Welcome people into the community—Any member who has been around for a while has context around the community's purpose, culture, and vibe. Help them help others figure out what's going on and how to plug in.

– Document community tools and processes—Especially in digital-first communities, it's important to write down information to keep people on the same page. Not only is it awesome for the documenter to be seen as a "keeper of wisdom," but writing down how something works is one of the most effective strategies to help others step into leadership.

When it comes to community contributions (a voluntary and opt-in exercise), leading with love is much more effective than being told what to do "or else."

That said, you can be strategic in how you use love to motivate people. For example, you might ask someone, "Do you think we can wrap up [project] today? You are the best," and follow up with, "Thanks again, [name]!" as a friendly reminder for them to complete it. If there still isn't any progress, you might ask people what resources and support they need, if they'd like to collaborate with another member, or if they'd like to pass ownership of the project to someone else. If it seems like someone's doubting their contribution to a project or their role on the team, write them a short letter expressing your gratitude for their work and dedication thus far.

Inclusion and trust are about enabling and recognizing contributions at all levels. It helps members see themselves as community stewards and practice leadership!

* * *

Decentralize Power

So, you've empowered community members to step up—now what? How do you supercharge their efforts and ensure they have everything they need to lead well?

In a typical school club, some things people need in order to be successful in a new leadership role include...

- A title/position in the community
- Strong relationships with club members
- Understanding of how different members relate to each other
- Context about the history and purpose of the club
- Tips from the previous leader in this role
- A handbook with key information they need to know
- Training to apply the ideas in the handbook

Indeed, when we look at how school clubs and organizations are passed on from one officer team to the next, it largely follows this pattern.

For example, I became a state officer for Washington Future Business Leaders of America (FBLA) in April 2017, when I was elected as the Southwest Region Vice President. One of the first things I received was the State Officer

Handbook, a binder of documents from the code of conduct to officer responsibilities. A couple weeks later, I participated in the state officer training, a three-day retreat where the team met each other and planned for the upcoming year. Throughout the year, I achieved my goals in part due to these officer trainings, and in part due to the strong relationships I had with fellow FBLA members in my region and across the country.

FBLA's process of empowering new leaders, which most other student organizations share, was complex and comprehensive. It ultimately achieved its intended purpose: All the officers knew what they should do, when they should do it, and how to go about doing it.

"So, what's the problem?" you might ask.

The process of selecting and empowering FBLA's newest leaders is incredibly top down. Resources are concentrated on a select few state officers. If you aren't elected, it often feels like you can't really *lead* in the FBLA community—and you probably wouldn't even have the resources to start. You wouldn't know which state officers to collaborate with, where to get funding, or how your initiatives tie into the organization's strategic priorities.

Instead of many FBLA members stepping up to assume leadership, whether that's creating competitive event resources or organizing networking events, everything falls on the state officers. Not only is this system stressful for officers, it also causes the organization to miss out on the collective energy, imagination, and leadership of its members.

Simply put, centralizing power holds back the growth of the community.

So how might we decentralize power and help everyone, regardless of title or length of membership or some other arbitrary identifier, take on leadership roles? It comes down to one thing: **reduce asymmetries**.

Joshua Vial, the co-founder of Enspiral, a self-described "network of people working on stuff that matters," writes about distributing leadership in *Better Work Together*. "As Enspiral started to gain traction, I had a very clear goal. I wanted a community of peers to engage with in a dance of dynamic leadership and followership," Vial said. Vial lives by the philosophy no one should lead all the time and everyone should lead some of the time. It's a great philosophy, but one that is hard to put into action due to asymmetries of power, information, relationships, skill, reputation, money, and time—all of which influence who can contribute and how effective they are.

For example, in the beginning of the community, Vial personally selected and onboarded new members. It created massive relational asymmetry. If anyone wanted to get connected with someone, they'd automatically seek out Vial because he had all of the intimate relationships. No one else was stepping up to introduce members and facilitate networking. If Vial disappeared, everything would collapse.

By noticing this asymmetry, Vial was able to create small interventions to reduce it, such as documenting the onboarding process and encouraging others to steward it.

There's a common misconception decentralizing power equates to a flat community where everyone is the same. Notice that's not what Vial was trying to do! Hierarchies exist for a reason; they help us uplift the people who care most about an issue, have the time and expertise to tackle it, and are willing to be held accountable to ensure progress is made.

Author and management consultant Gary Hamel writes in *Humanocracy*, "On any issue some colleagues will have a bigger say than others will, depending on their expertise and willingness to help. These are hierarchies of influence, not position, and they're built from the bottom up." The key is instead of a single formal hierarchy, we want lots of informal, evolving, overlapping ones—based on passions, strengths, and expertise. When the right opportunity emerges, every member should have ample support and resources to contribute their gifts to serve the community. So, what conditions allow these naturally dynamic hierarchies to form?

Removing Titles

One of the simplest strategies to create an environment more conducive to informal hierarchies is by removing formal, dominant ones: titles.

Titles can come with a lot of baggage. When I first joined clubs in high school, I was honestly surprised by how important titles felt. People introduced themselves using their titles, which made me (as someone who didn't have one) feel out of place and like I didn't belong. Even worse, titles give certain people permission to contribute while barring everyone else. For example, although I loved spreadsheets and organizing events, I never helped organize any of Key Club's service events… I didn't want to step on the secretary's toes or imply they were doing a bad job.

As a result, I became obsessed with titles. I was hyper-aware of what everyone's titles were and my relation to them. Depending on their title and my title (or lack thereof), I was more hesitant to share new ideas or challenge existing assumptions. I started to collect titles, which I thought was a prerequisite to making meaningful community contributions... and once I got the title, the roles flipped. I went around flaunting my title as a pass to create change: "Hi, I'm the director of _____. It's why I have access to this space, and now I'm here to save the day!" I started to realize titles are not just harmful for new members of the community, but also those with titles themselves, who have an inflated sense of importance. Remember, if the community is contingent on you, it's not a community! Titles are dangerous all around.

Later on, I realized why titles felt so serious: It's the way young people are recognized for their contributions. It made me wonder: Are there more fluid ways to recognize and appreciate the people in our communities who step up? How might we transition into new ways of acknowledging leaders?

Here are some ideas to consider:

- **Digital tokens of appreciation.** Civics Unplugged uses the HeyTaco! plugin in Slack. Each community member has five tacos to give away to others every day and can easily do that by tagging their name in the appreciation message.
- **Describe how people add value.** Titles are shortcuts that simplify what members bring to a community. How else do you describe everything someone does in a two- or three-word title? Instead of defaulting to a role, help people describe their contributions instead. For example, instead of being the "director of partnerships," a community member might "lead the partnership with _____ in order to _____." Titles grant clout, but not everyone can be a director of something. If you truly want to empower every member to lead, you'll need to help them describe how they add value using numbers and stories, which are infinite.

- **Model the way.** People look to community builders for cues on how to act. If you move away from status-signaling language, you'll inspire others to do so as well! It's especially powerful when high-status community members (founders, long-time members, accomplished people) describe themselves as simply "members" or "friends" or some other shared identifier. For example, folks in Civics Unplugged's community are all called *Builders!*

If you're reading this and feel removing titles isn't realistic for your community, there's another alternative: creative and uncommon titles that don't imply hierarchy. These titles can be everything from "Community Empowerment Associate" to "Operations Ninja" in less formal scenarios. Instead of presidents and vice presidents, you might remove the part of the title that broadcasts rank and instead highlight what people do ("vice president of marketing" → "head of marketing" or "marketing lead"). Any change that creates space for informal hierarchies to emerge is a step in the right direction.

Balance Asymmetries

As mentioned earlier, one of the biggest barriers to decentralizing power are the asymmetries that exist between community members, which can lead to unintended power-over dynamics.

For example, founders have incredible power in new communities. Why? It might be because they have...

- Context behind the community and the various projects happening within it, so they know how members can plug in.

- Understanding of the community's evolutionary purpose and long-term vision, so they know whether new ideas fit into the community's strategic priorities.
- Relationships with a broad swath of members, so anyone who wants to organize cross-team projects needs to ask the founder to facilitate the connection.

These challenges are things I experienced when I founded Project Exchange in 2018. Even before onboarding the first team member, I'd spent months thinking about the idea. Everything was in my head: the vision for the community, what our key initiatives would be, and who we needed to get on board.

Later that year, I reviewed applications, interviewed candidates, and personally onboarded our first team members, board of director members, and even our early students. Because I had such a great understanding of the strategic vision and each person's contribution, I assigned discrete, weekly tasks people could do. Team members never got to know each other or the community's long-term vision.

It's clear now the reason I was powerful was because I unintentionally preserved asymmetries of information and relationships. Community builders must consciously speak about and manage these asymmetries. If we don't, power will remain concentrated with "high-status" members and everyone else will find it hard to step up and lead.

Here are some common asymmetries and steps you might take to address them:

- **Information.** Founding and older members can have more context about the community: why it was created, how it has changed, current projects and their statuses, and short- and long-term goals. Consider creating white-papers, newsletters, or even a content index of inspirations that captures your community's evolution and thought process.

- **Relationships.** Extroverted members, or folks who are heavily involved in community member recruitment, selection, and onboarding processes have a disproportionate number and depth of relationships within the community. Consider creating member directories, one-to-one and small group networking events, and simple processes to facilitate personal introductions between members whose work and interests align (maybe there's a template people can use to make intros for each other)!

- **Skill.** Older members or those with industry/academic experience will often have more expertise in certain areas the community needs help with. It's a good thing to have these folks around! Facilitate mentor-mentee matches, develop skill-sharing workshops, or even organize cohort-based STEVEs (like the ones discussed in Chapter 2.5) to help new members gain the knowledge they need to contribute as well.

If your community is asymmetrical, it's not the end of the world. Acknowledging asymmetries and unequal power distribution is the first step in addressing them.

Along the way, engage in meta-reflection. Observe your own actions within the community and talk about your power and status with others—it shouldn't be a taboo topic! As a "high status" community member, your intention to step back and devolve power can catalyze a positive chain reaction.

Documentation

Finally, many of the strategies to reduce community asymmetries include some form of documentation.

Communities are complex, living gardens. Just like how garden tenders balance many tasks at once—watering and feeding plants, trimming and pruning, even subtle things like adding visitor signs to ensure the garden is flourishing—community builders do as well. They need to consider everything from member preferences to community rituals to trends in the larger world, in order to make optimal decisions for their community.

Because so much is involved in caring for a garden, most of us do not know how and don't volunteer to either. We might fear we'd create more harm than good or simply embarrass ourselves in the process. A gardener's handbook encourages visitors to overcome fear and step into leadership.

Putting together a handbook seems obvious, yet it's often neglected by community builders who deem it too extra, too formal, and too much work.

Instead, people resort to syncing on a regular basis. It's pretty obvious why mental syncing is not enough unless you have telepathic abilities. Verbal syncing becomes a game of telephone in groups larger than two. Add the fact you're tending a digital-first community with members all over the place, you have a recipe for an uncoordinated community full of confusion. Delegation of responsibilities are vague, work is duplicated, and people constantly drop the ball… Your community simply isn't effective without a handbook.

How might we go about creating one?

First, consider the information you want to include. The goal is to make it easy for anyone to be able to figure out things like...

- **Inspirations and influences**. What people, content, or other communities have influenced the design of your own? Not only is this information very telling about the vibe and purpose of your community, it's a great way to capture the thought and intention that went into creating it.
- **Tools**. Technology plays a huge role in digital communities and can be new or hard to navigate. That's why a whole chapter in this book is dedicated to exploring various community platforms! Documenting what tools your community uses and how you use them can help increase member effectiveness and collaboration.
- **Key objectives and design choices**. Create documents that outline key objectives, design choices, and potential pitfalls for your community's core events, projects, and practices. Design docs serve as a forcing function for you to explain why something in your community is designed a certain way, how it serves members, and realizes your community's purpose. It makes it easy for new leaders to iterate on old initiatives and create new ones with the insight from previous experiments.
- **Processes**. Popular phrases like "The journey is more important than the destination" and "The means do not justify the ends" speak to the importance of process: *how* you achieve something is just as important, if not more so, than what you achieve. Almost every community activity has an associated process, whether that's how you onboard new members or address conflicts. Processes form the bulk of your documentation. By writing down

the how, you make it easy for processes to be replicated, examined, and evolved by new members, not just the people who created them.

One of the best ways to tackle documentation is by embedding it into a group process, instead of treating it as an inconvenient add-on. For example, you might encourage members to engage in regular group reflections where you work together to document what your community has learned, how it has grown, where you are now, and where you want to go. Having a facilitator take notes during meetings or a visual storyteller who documents themes in real time is a powerful way to preserve key insights for future members.

As you do this, remember: Start small and make sure your documentation is easily accessible and searchable, so it's used by members.

In the *Checklist Manifesto*, surgeon, writer, and public health researcher Atul Gawande describes how checklists (a form of documentation) can even help experts—the oldest, most dedicated community members—remember how to steward a complex process or system. Gawande emphasizes above all, documentation should be practical. It should be precise, to the point, and only include the most important steps.

Documentation isn't intended to be intrusive. Rather, it supplements the knowledge and judgment of long-time leaders by preserving community processes, how it has evolved over time, and how it maps to community goals.

At the end of the day, it's impossible for you, a single community steward, to do everything alone. A core objective of both leading with love and decentralizing power is to make it easier for new members to step up and help steward your community. People are hesitant to step up if they aren't invited and supported—for example, I would *never* touch my neighbor's garden for fear I trim a plant incorrectly, especially if it seems like my neighbor has an emotional mom-like relationship to the garden.

One of the biggest challenges, and biggest opportunities, is for community builders to share power. You'll know you've succeeded when the community starts running on its own!

3.1

QUALITIES OF A GOOD COMMUNITY BUILDER

———

"There will always be people telling you what you're supposed to be doing, but you have to question that. People feel lost when there are no clear models to show them what to feel or what to experiment with. I heard once that there are three stages in an artist's search. One is imitation—imitating everything that you think is cool and groovy, and you want to identify with. Then once you imitate, you take those imitations and you experiment with blending and exploring—that's the second stage. And then the third stage is self-realization and self-discovery. Discovering your own language and your own voice out of all the experimentation and imitation you've been working at... Finding your own voice and your own language, even if it takes years to do it, is such a good feeling. It's the best."

—LARAAJI

As a child, no one ever told me, "You know, Ashley, I think you'll grow up to be a great community builder." Not even close.

At school, I was the quiet kid. I wasn't especially funny, hung out at the edges of a room, and would hesitate at the classroom door before mustering up the courage to step inside on the first day of class. Whenever the teacher unleashed us to find group project partners, without fail, I was the last person to jump into the fray. In fact, I'd often skip class on the days we found partners, knowing the teacher would assign me a group or I could just do the project on my own.

Because of my actions, those around me (and eventually myself) excluded me from being a community builder. I was not extroverted, super talkative, or the life of the party. If I can't even make small talk for ten minutes, how can I build community? Instead, the people pegged as good community builders are associated student body (ASB) archetypes: the people who are super popular, confident, have lots of friends, participate in numerous clubs on campus, and bring high energy wherever they go. And sure, ASB types can become great community builders, but that archetype isn't me—and it's not many other people either.

Here's the good news: nowhere in this book does it say good community builders must be super popular, confident, or able to make small talk for ten minutes.

A common misconception exists that community builders are like ASB kids. It's tempting to exclude yourself from community building if you don't quite fit the mold, but there's a big flaw to that mindset. Every person—introverted or extroverted, quiet or talkative, life of the party or not—needs community. Because we all crave community-like spaces, we intuitively know what good ones feel like and have the capacity to create them for ourselves and others like us. Introverts understand other introverts best and consider community design choices extroverts might not even think about!

Sure, a number of qualities make some people more effective community builders than others such as effective dialogue facilitation, clear technical writing, and established knowledge of community tech platforms. However, these skills can be cultivated over time. You can also find co-founders and community members with complementary skills to supplement ones you lack. Effective documentation of your community's core structures and processes help fill in the rest.

So, if you've never thought of yourself as a community builder, think again.

There are only three hard requirements all community builders need: time, emotional maturity, and a chip on the shoulder.

* * *

Three Minimum Requirements

Instead of trying to measure how qualified you are to start a digital community (if we all waited until we were 100 percent "ready," the community would never get started!), measure whether you have the capacity and bandwidth to tend to your community in the long run:

- **Time**. Community building does not happen by magic. You'll need to follow specific steps, like finding people and choosing technology—all of which require time and energy.

- **Emotional maturity.** Self-awareness and confidence help you generate surplus energy to serve others. Surplus energy then allows you to expand your sense of self and bring the right vibe into a space.
- **A chip on your shoulder.** A spark—a problem you've faced, an injustice you've witnessed—inspires you to start the community. This spark sustains your motivation in the face of obstacles throughout the community building process.

It's important to note these are not personality traits, but rather qualities *anyone* can cultivate. Whether you have time is not something static. You can choose to create time for the things you love, like starting or stewarding a community, by prioritizing it and stepping back from other responsibilities.

Time

This element is perhaps one of the most intuitive requirements for community building. Before you set out to build a community, ensure you can dedicate enough time to growing and stewarding it, especially in its early phases.

Rushing community building can have very negative consequences. You might skip a critical step, like finding your people, and end up designing transformative experiences without any members to actually experience them. You might select the wrong tech platform(s), forget to create rules, unintentionally centralize power by avoiding documentation, or something else entirely. Each step in the community building process builds on the next. Corners are not meant to be cut!

As you've seen throughout the book, community isn't something that happens on its own. People do many things to lay the foundation for community, from designing community agreements to planning rituals that transform members. These milestones are slow and steady. Successful communities are created through deep reflection (like answering the questions in the Community Canvas Guidebook), empathetic conversations, and many feedback-iteration cycles. Relationships, trust, and discovering your community's purpose are all things that take time.

Just like you can't throw seeds in dirt and expect a beautiful garden to form overnight and sustain itself, you can't start a Slack channel and expect a community to magically organize. If you treat your garden like a once-and-done thing, your plants will die because they didn't receive the nutrients/resources/conditions needed to thrive. The same thing happens in communities. Energy is dispersed, conversation withers away, and people phase out. It's important to remember community building is a long-term investment over weeks and months.

At the beginning of my journey, I fell into the trap of putting softer community interactions like welcoming people or asking how they're doing in the "if time allows" category (time usually did not allow). It's easy to de-prioritize small and seemingly insignificant actions, not realizing communities are built on the micro moments in between big, sparkly events. I've found it helpful to block time on my calendar dedicated to tending communities and checking in with members.

Another trap people fall into when thinking about community is that because it's a "fun thing" and fun things aren't work, community building won't *really* take up time and energy. Yes, communities are fun, healing, and energizing (they're supposed to be!)—but they don't form on their own. Communities reflect the energy participants infuse into them. In this way, community building is just like any other project. There's an upfront investment of your time, and you get out what you put in. If you don't invest in your community, you're going to have a dysfunctional group of people hanging together by a thread. But for the right person, creating a community is a special opportunity, and a potentially life-changing one.

So, be real with yourself. Do you have enough time to make this community the best it can be?

The number of hours community builders need varies, depending on the person and the type of community they're trying to create. That said, if you can't commit at least three hours each week to interact with community members and carry out recurring community practices, it probably doesn't make sense for you to start one right now. Consider joining an adjacent community as a member instead, finding a co-founder, or simply sharing your idea so others might see it and decide to take initiative. As author and former dot-com business executive Seth Godin says, "Ideas in secret die. They need light and air, or they starve to death." If you don't have the bandwidth to build a community, the next best option is to find someone similarly capable, committed, and passionate about your cause!

Here's what to **not** do: Stay up until 3 a.m. every day to tend to your community. You'll only run yourself ragged and transfer that energy to the group. Community building is all about vibe curation, and a burnt-out vibe is not where it's at!

If you *really* want to steward a community and don't have time, you'll need to create time. This often means saying "no" to other commitments.

Emotional Maturity

In her book *Belong*, Radha Agarwal argues you cannot truly discover or create thriving communities if you haven't first figured out who **you** are. Without gentle self-awareness—a good understanding of your values, interests, and passions—it's hard to know *what* communities you need, much less create them. Agarwal says going IN and developing an honest understanding of yourself allows you to get intentional about what you want and the skills you have to get there. After you learn to lead yourself, you can go OUT and get people together. Without doing the inner work to figure out who you are and why you show up, you won't be able to identify what really matters.

So, what does "knowing yourself" mean? It's *emotional maturity*—and not just about managing emotions and keeping your cool.

In an address delivered to the Institute on Nursing Education in 1948, Franz Alexander described emotional maturity as overcoming insecurity and developing confidence by taking oneself and one's capacities for granted. Alexander says young adults are "biologically full-grown but in many respects still children. One has the impression they do not know what to do with themselves in their newly acquired status." This insecurity manifests as self-consciousness, excessive competitiveness, boastfulness, awkwardness, and instability. As you can imagine, these are traits we do not want to bring into our communities.

Adolescence—the period of time when young people experience significant change and start to prove themselves—facilitates the development of inner security and confidence. And once young people develop emotional maturity, their interests no longer center around themselves. They start expanding their sense of self and directing energy to serve others.

Maturity manifests as positive surplus energy. This notion is critical because as you saw in Chapter 2.6 on capturing vibe, community architecture is thoughtful energy curation. Positive energy breeds positive community. The energy community builders bring is priceless and one of the most effective levers of change. Positive surplus energy results in increased...

- **Generosity.** The person is no longer primarily a receiver. They have energy that can be applied creatively to positively impact other people. Mature people can give without expecting something in return.
- **Growth.** The person has a realistic understanding of their own strengths and opportunities for development. They seek challenging perspectives, adjust based on feedback, and adapt to change.
- **Responsibility.** The person is no longer seeking external validation. Combined with intimate knowledge of themselves and their work, this mindset allows mature people to take ownership for and accept the consequences of their actions.

It's hard to say when someone has "enough" emotional maturity to start a community. These aren't binary qualities. Take generosity for instance: generosity is a spectrum. It's a virtue to live by, not a goal to be reached. At times, I am stingy. Other times, I am overly extravagant. It often depends on the person I'm speaking to or the specific situation I'm in. By maintaining self-awareness, reflecting on performance, and forgiving mistakes, I can become my best self.

Awareness is the first step to emotional maturity.

If this knowledge is new to you, do not worry! Consider finding an accountability buddy and syncing once a week to reflect on the energy you bring into a community. You can even ask for direct feedback from certain community members. Getting outside perspectives and constantly reflecting on how you show up is key.

A Chip On Your Shoulder

A chip on your shoulder attracts a negative connotation but might actually be a healthy thing to have. Angela Duckworth, author of the *New York Times* bestselling book *Grit*, argues many of the grittiest people have chips on their shoulders. In an interview with the Seattle Seahawks' coach, Pete Carroll, Duckworth discusses how the athlete's chip drives motivation and turns a player from good to great.

"The guys that really have grit, the mindset that they're always going to succeed, that have something to prove, they're resilient, they're not going to let setbacks hold them back, they're not going to be deterred by challenges and hurdles," says Carroll. "When you have that, you overcome a lot."

The strongest communities form around these challenges. A chip on your shoulder gives purpose to a community.

As you develop emotional maturity, you'll discover your unique set of values, strengths, passions, and long-term goals. You might discover things that frustrate you or things you yearn for. You'll start to notice everyone around you who has those same frustrations and yearnings. Odds are, it's more than just you! If you aren't able to find existing communities that address a problem you've personally experienced, that is one of the best signals to start your own.

Let the problem serve as a "chip on your shoulder"—something that sparks your motivation to start the community. It can be an injustice, an unexpected event, another problem you deeply empathize with. For example, maybe your chip is there's no safe space to talk about mental health during quarantine because you're stuck at home and family members can't relate. Or maybe it's feeling sluggish throughout the day because early morning swim team practices no longer exist.

When community builders have a chip on their shoulders, they are more likely to...

- **Sustain energy and excitement**. Starting a community is a long process. It requires time, energy, and resilience when things flop—and believe me, things flop. There will be Zoom meetings where no one shows up, periods of awkward silence, and instances when you send the wrong calendar invite. It's a lot easier to stay excited if you start off with a clear, strong reason why this community needs to exist.
- **Attract new members.** When your community stands for something, it's a lot more attractive to prospective community members and supporters. Without a central message explaining why a community exists, it's hard to justify investing time, energy, and resources to help it grow.
- **Learn the skills they need**. People who have a personal connection to the problem their community addresses have a reason to remain curious and learn whatever is needed to help their community. People with chips on their shoulders have a natural incentive to cultivate skills like social media marketing and dialogue facilitation if it means helping their community move forward.

To figure out if you have a chip on your shoulder, ask yourself: Why am I starting this community in the first place? If you don't know the answer, consider going back to step two and go IN to identify what you care about. Remember self-awareness and getting people together is an ongoing process. At any point, if you no longer feel a sense of urgency and personal connection, it may make sense to pass on the role to someone else.

Time, emotional maturity, and a chip on the shoulder are the necessary requirements to lead a community. Everything else is learned along the way or even delegated to others. Once you cultivate these three qualities in yourself, it's time to move on to the next part: apply community building knowledge into your existing groups!

3.2

CULTURE CHANGER

"In times of change, learners inherit the earth, while the learned find themselves beautifully equipped to deal with a world that no longer exists."

—ERIC HOFFER

Let's say you have the minimum requirements a community builder needs: time, emotional maturity, and a chip on the shoulder. Your next question might be, "Well, *should* I start a digital-first community?"

There's a lot of pressure today for young people to start things. Everyone is the founder of this, or the CEO of that. Slapping "community" on your youth-led initiative is a way to make it sound nicer and signal your impressive maturity level—you're thinking about your peers! To be fair, there are completely valid reasons for starting a new digital-first community, and using youth-led initiatives for personal gain isn't always mutually exclusive with positive impact. But for the majority of us, we won't start new communities (and we shouldn't let external pressure compel us to do so). There's no need to pour your energy and time into starting something that meets a nonexistent need.

I'll also state the obvious: You're already part of many groups, most of which could be more community-like! They can be improved with your time, energy, and imagination.

Young people acquire leadership positions and are involved with many things outside of school. At various points in my formative high school years, I was part of the swim team, STEM Academy (a club that organized monthly STEM activities for students at the local elementary school), Key Club, FBLA, and more. My friends did ASB, speech and debate, National Honor Society, and the yearbook team. For some of us, these clubs were true communities, but more often than not, they completely miss the mark. Instead, they're simply extracurriculars we trudge through.

Imagine if every one of your activities was a real community. How would that increase your mental and emotional well-being? Your productivity? Your love for fellow community members and the world? Your commitment to showing up as your best self? Your excitement about and hope for the future?

Being part of flourishing communities puts you on an upward trajectory.

There's no reason why you should resign yourself to groups that aren't community-like. You can take concrete steps today to make your friend groups, sports teams, school clubs, nonprofit organizations, and other extracurriculars more community-spirited, without starting a new community of your own. This chapter shares some of those action steps!

* * *

Gentle Wins the Game

Just like how community isn't created overnight, changing your community's culture also does not happen overnight. Especially if your club/team/organization (let's call it "Group") has existed for a while, you're up against a distinct non-community-like culture. Maybe no one in your Group turns on their cameras during Zoom meetings, meeting agendas are very top down and bureaucratic, or the Slack channel is inactive. It's still possible to evolve your Group to become more community-like, but there's extra activation energy needed to overcome the challenges your Group faces.

If community members show up in your community's Slack tomorrow and everything has changed—titles are removed, there's no meeting agenda, ten new community rituals are instated—members will (understandably) be very confused.

Beyond creating confusion, introducing changes to your Group too quickly may alienate community members who are used to the status quo. Changes could simply be so different from the Group's current vibe that no one knows how to show up anymore, especially if people haven't experienced true community before. Move too fast, and you risk losing people along the transition.

Of course, it's impossible to not lose people along the way. It's important to think of your dual roles as the caretakers for the old culture in your community, and the pioneers for the new one. Instead of breaking everything down and re-building anew (which requires your community to go through a period of chaos with undefined culture), shift your Group's culture *gradually*. Gentle experiments help everyday members feel acknowledged and supported along the way, give people time to adjust to new ways of showing up in the community, and empower them to be part of the community's transformation.

Here's what the arc of gentle culture evolution might look like:

Co-create a New Vision

Before you jump into action, it's important to remember you're not a dictator. Instead of telling people what to do and where the community is headed, actively work alongside members to envision the future you want to build. There is no need to make sure people are aligned on the vision, because they played a role in creating it! Part of this process requires acknowledgement that the community can be and needs to improve—and that members have unique insight on where improvements are needed most.

As true co-creators, community members are invited to offer advice, ask clarifying questions, and introduce provocations. They have a deep understanding of why changes are being made and how they will be part of it. Without co-creation, it's hard to get people to buy in, much less contribute to change. Individual members might work to make the community culture "better," but fail to make progress or gain momentum without getting others on board. Folks might even have opposite definitions of a better culture and take actions that cancel each other out!

Introduce Small Experiments

Any kind of change starts with a bold vision and people who take initiative to turn it into reality. Experimentation allows communities to test ideas and discover more effective ways of doing things. Ideal experiments are low-risk, high-reward opportunities free of pressure to succeed. Optimal experiments present valuable insights in spite of failure. They often help community members understand what the new culture feels like, provide feedback, and inform new iterations of community practices. Experimentation reminds people they are in control of the process and changing community culture doesn't mean it will become unrecognizable overnight or disappear altogether.

Engage in Observation and Reflection

Making observations is a powerful strategy to help community members gain self-awareness and shift group dynamics toward a new culture. You might say, "I noticed we've created a norm of not having our video on during team meetings... Is this the kind of vibe we want to create? How did this happen? What actions can we take to ensure we are building the kind of vibe we want?" You can also observe the emotional reaction someone has to an experiment, or the tensions and commonalities that emerge. An observation might be, "It seems like everyone enjoyed the new icebreaker platform we tried out."

The key to making the most of observation is to reflect on it immediately after one is made. Reflection invites feedback from community members and makes transforming culture more participatory. It empowers people to take initiative and lead small experiments, or simply be more active participants within them. As a bonus, reflection creates space for you and members to set expectations of each other and the community as a whole. It's a natural check-in point to ensure everyone is aligned on the new vision!

* * *

Ideas for Small Experiments

Small experiments refer to discrete practices, rituals, and events that can easily be tried out once or twice, or for a short period of time. They create an easy way for community members to experience firsthand what "more community-like" means and whether it's something they can get behind.

It's no surprise people are resistant to change. By framing something as a time-bound experiment, people are more likely to support it. What often happens is members become so obsessed with these experiences they want more of them, which accelerates the community's transformation!

The most successful experiments I've observed fall into three categories: evolving how your community executes synchronous meetings, introducing new rituals, and creating events that embody the culture you're trying to put in place.

Meetings

Unsurprisingly, meetings are one of the key ways digital-first communities stay connected—seeing someone's face via

Zoom is one of the closest experiences we have to mirror real-life interactions. Most online communities already have some sort of recurring synchronous meeting that helps people stay connected.

That said, even the word "meeting" doesn't sound very exciting, which makes them one of the best places to shift culture. Meetings are repeated consistently, and people are often more than willing to try something new. What are the different ways your community might structure and lead meetings? How might you make them more opt-in, fun, and spontaneous?

Depending on the vibe you're hoping to create, consider...

- **Switching up the technology**—If everyone has their Zoom video off and that creates disconnection, maybe suggest a meeting on another platform. Gatheraround or Around The World facilitate one-to-one and small group speed rounds, where folks are more likely to turn on video. Alternatively, you might experiment with Zoom chat, polls, or audio-first platforms like Discord's voice channels to boost member engagement.

- **Asking how people are doing**—It's easy to get caught up in the agenda and completely forget the human aspects of meetings. People tend to remember the beginning and end of meetings the most, so consider using the first or last five minutes to connect with members beyond a routine "how are you?"—even if it's just taking an extra moment to acknowledge the other person's response. Alternatively, you might start the meeting with a short meditation, breakout rooms and a personal question, or invite people to drop an emoji in the chat that describes how they're feeling.

- **Embracing silence**—Silence isn't necessarily a bad thing. Sometimes it means people are thinking or reflecting! Encourage your facilitators to give people time to process before they respond or move on to the next item.
- **Going agenda-free or slides-free**—While having an agenda or slides can make us feel "prepared," sometimes they can hold the group back. You'd be surprised by the brilliant insights shared when members are given the freedom to discuss whatever feels meaningful. This strategy is especially useful in dialogue-centered meetings, like brainstorming sessions. Trust the process and see where the group goes! If you aren't ready to go fully agenda-free, consider a less rigid agenda or invite members to add agenda items at the beginning of the meeting to create group buy-in.

Remember, you can make small experiments less awkward (especially ones like asking how people are doing and sitting in silence) by explicitly stating and explaining why this is something you're trying. Throughout the process, observation and reflection is key!

And if the experiment creates an unintended outcome, there's no need to stress. After all, it is just an experiment.

Rituals

As you've come to learn, rituals are things your community does over and over with intention—making them the perfect place to plant seeds for your Group's new culture.

Rituals vary dramatically based on the vibe you're trying to create. Brainstorm with community members. Ask folks what they enjoy doing, what could be made one hundred times better if done with people instead of alone, and what aligns most closely with your community's vision. Then, explore how you might do these things with intention, attention, and repetition.

If you're looking for ideas, some rituals include…

- **Community reflection threads**—Create a daily or weekly reflection prompt members can respond to in Slack or a similar platform and get to know each other. Reflection threads give people an excuse to connect (starting conversations can feel awkward), and move conversations towards personal experiences and feelings, which facilitates deeper connection.
- **Shoutouts and gratitude**—What better way is there to help people feel seen and appreciated, than by publicly recognizing their contributions? In Civics Unplugged's Slack channel, weekly Sunday Shoutout posts encourage community members to shout out a personal accomplishment and a fellow community member for something awesome they did. For example, one Builder wrote, "@ xxx- For one of my scholarship applications I was asked to write about an act of patriotism that inspires me, and I chose to write about you and Bloom. I was awarded the scholarship today, and I just wanted to tell you you're a cool human who's doing cool things." Needless to say, it made that person's day.
- **Art and movement**—Another strategy is to create rituals that foster deep connection by incorporating art (poem, music, a piece of writing) or movement (breathwork, meditation, breakout dance). An article in the *Scientific American* explains how "crew rowing, line dancing, choir

singing or simply tapping fingers in sync increase generosity, trust, and tolerance toward others" and help us create stronger social bonds. Shared art and movement unites the community.

Events

Last but not least, hosting one-off events. Events have the potential to recur, given enough community interest, and are one of the most effective ways to keep your community engaged. They also represent a catch-all way to present new experiments and engage members in the process.

When designing community events, think about how they make people feel. Do people feel connected, understood, and accepted? The best events include opportunities for members to...

- **Connect 1:1 or in small groups**—It's easy for members to get lost as your community grows. Small groups are where connections of care are formed. Consider hosting events like PowerPoint nights, scavenger hunts, and bake offs that help people get to know each other in new, playful environments. Platforms like Gatheraround and Glimpse make it easy to create speed-dating style events between members. Initiatives like peer accountability buddies or mentorship programs also foster intimate connection.
- **Talk, vent, make sense of the world**—It can sometimes feel like every community event is about content. We think the best way to support people is to give them tools and more tools, when in reality, people just want a place to make sense of the world and feel connected to others.

Any dialogue event that invites people to talk about "whatever feels meaningful" and has a facilitator to hold space is a surefire way to help people feel acknowledged and like they belong.

- **Solve a problem together**—Few things bring people closer together than working on a meaningful project and creating something useful. For example, organize mutual aid circles, problem-solving workshops, or even mini hackathons, where members bring a challenge they are facing and harness the community's knowledge and resources to address it. Chill co-working or brainstorming sessions are also good places to start.

Ultimately, any of these practices emerge in your community as a gentle experiment—you shouldn't feel bad if one goes wrong or doesn't work out. That's the whole point! You might experiment with a short questionnaire to screen prospective members, ask for volunteers to facilitate weekly community calls, or start a meme channel in Slack and invite members to contribute. Start by making a list of possible experiments for the community, and if you feel lost, ask members to contribute ideas.

What makes an experiment gentle is not *what* the experiment is, but rather how you approach it. Advance the experiment with moderation (start small) and propose it as an option to your community (instead of a requirement). Let your community determine which experiments persist or perish. Through small experiments, everyday members have the power to create change from the inside and make their existing Groups more community-like.

Helping your existing Groups evolve is incredibly important—but if you're looking to design a space from the ground up and tackle a *who* or *why* not addressed by existing communities, you'll want to create new ones. To go one step further and start digital-first communities of your own, read on!

3.3

NEW COMMUNITY BUILDER

———

"Our deepest fear is not that we are inadequate. Our deepest fear is that we are powerful beyond measure... As we let our own light shine, we unconsciously give other people permission to do the same. As we are liberated from our own fear, our presence automatically liberates others."

—MARIANNE WILLIAMSON

Apart from making an existing Group more community-like, another option you may choose to take is to start your own digital-first community!

There are valid reasons to start something new. Maybe your community idea tackles a problem that is currently neglected, takes a different approach to solving it, or targets a demographic currently neglected. It's wise to create communities that address a need you've personally experienced, especially if you can't find an existing one that does so. Building your community from the ground up gives you a unique opportunity to design the community you need and ensures it's structures and practices values and purpose-aligned.

For the right person, starting a community is an incredibly rewarding experience. It's one of the best ways to connect with people who have a similar chip on their shoulder. By starting a community, you can directly address a need you and others share. You'll shape solutions, bring them into the world, affect the lives of real people, and in the process, make your own personal discoveries.

As you know, we don't have enough flourishing digital-first communities in a time when they're needed most. Young people are spending increasing amounts of time on digital devices. Simultaneously, we're seeing a rise in loneliness and mental health issues, alongside critical global issues that require cross-sector, multi-stakeholder coordination to create solutions. Meaningful connections and trust-building through online communities help tackle these issues.

More importantly, there are too few spaces in the world where young people have agency to make decisions that shape the future. The world is often something that happens to us, instead of something we have control over. We don't realize when we get together in a spirit of generosity—circulate information, share resources, make sense of the world together—we have more power than we realize.

To put this concept into context: I share an idea. Harmonie adds something to it. Stella poses a provocation that inspires us to go in a new direction. Then, we create a small experiment and try it together. I realize I have a mentor who might have insights to share. Harmonie suggests a grant opportunity. Pretty soon, we've successfully created something none of us could have created by ourselves.

We're so busy waiting for the adult or the big donor to empower us we forget we already have everything we need in our communities!

* * *

Asking the Right Questions

There are many great reasons to start a digital-first community, but there are also a few pitfalls to consider.

Some people believe starting a community is the only way to address a problem. They decide to start a new digital-first community, even when joining and supporting an existing one is more effective. They don't realize more communities can create confusion, duplicate work, and siphon resources from (perhaps more effective) existing communities working to solve the same problem.

Others believe starting a community could only be a positive experience, so it must be the right choice. Even if the three minimum requirements of a good community builder are unmet (time, emotional maturity, and a chip on their shoulder), these people believe they are well-positioned to start one anyway. By diving in too early without the necessary qualifications, they struggle to start, much less sustain and scale, a flourishing community.

Yes, building community is a learning process. You don't need to know *everything* nor have all the skills required;

that's where collaboration comes into play. But the qualities of a good community builder cannot be glossed over.

To avoid the pitfalls above, here are two questions to consider before you commit to the process.

1. Does this community need to exist, and if so, why online?

When quarantine first started in March 2020, I was determined to migrate every community I belonged to online, for the sake of normalcy. I didn't pause to consider how people's needs and priorities evolve, making some of these communities no longer relevant. For example, I was determined to host FBLA meetings and the state conference. I prodded people around me to make it happen—even when I knew deep down others were more concerned about their mental health than competitive events.

Furthermore, some things just aren't meant to happen online. Just think about moving swim practice to a video conference call... Good luck.

That said, digital-first creates many opportunities to reimagine what your community does together. Let's use the swim team community as an example. If swim team members largely bond in person over morning practice—waking up early, doing something focused and physically exhausting together—maybe the group decides to wake up at 6 a.m. for online Zoom yoga and meditation sessions! Or maybe yoga and meditation sessions don't resonate, and you realize needs have evolved. People might have gained appreciation for sleep and self-care during quarantine and are searching for simpler ways to stay connected, like an Instagram group chat or spontaneous Zoom movie nights.

If that iteration doesn't work, go back to swim team members and ask them what they're looking for. Are they missing the team? How would they like to stay connected? What feels meaningful and joyful right now?

As you evaluate whether a certain digital-first community needs to exist, consider whether...

- **Your community addresses a unique need that others do not**—How is your community different from all the other ones vying for our attention? Remember: differences can be based on your community's *why* or *who*. Two communities might share the same why, but have different barriers to entry and vibe, which attracts different people. Being aware of similar or adjacent communities prevents you from duplicating effort, helps you guide people toward a space that's best for them, and may even lead to collaboration down the road.
- **You can think of five friends who'd be a "hell yeah" to join the community**—This is a good test to see if your community idea is viable. Do you know anyone who is excited about something like this? If so, reach out and ask them to be your founding community members! If you receive a negative response (or can't think of anyone to reach out to), go back to the drawing board and iterate on your community's why and who.

2. Why am I the right person to start and steward this community?

The community builder is critically important for a community's stability. Ideally you become less important as the community matures and power decentralizes—but in the early stages, you provide activation energy that gets the community off the ground. Founding community members will likely be *your* close friends. Event facilitation is only as good as *you* make it. Even the rules sound like they're written by you (with input from members, of course).

Needless to say, starting out with the right community builder is one of the most critical determinants of community success. A huge component of community builder fit is how deeply you empathize with and understand the problem your community hopes to tackle.

Having a chip on your shoulder is great, but passion must be combined with reason to create change. You need to think analytically about creating tangible outcomes. For example, you may have already...

- Taken action to understand the problem more deeply
- Mobilized friends and family to take actions with you
- Identified how tending this community aligns with your values, strengths, passions, and long-term goals
- Discovered inspiring and encouraging role models working in a similar problem space

I spent a significant chunk of my high school career building Project Exchange's global community of high school and college students passionate about making study abroad more accessible through online cultural exchange. My chip on the shoulder was experiencing the problem firsthand—study abroad experiences cost thousands of dollars and were financially infeasible for my family.

But I didn't stop there: I served as a 2018 U.S. Youth Ambassador to Uruguay and experienced firsthand why study abroad is so important. It isn't just an opportunity to make friends and have a good time, but to work with different people to tackle global issues. I mobilized people by sharing my experience in Uruguay and organizing an experiment which introduced American and Uruguayan friends via text message for a mini exchange, like the WhatsApp conversation I had with my host family pre-departure. I identified why this project felt so meaningful: I deeply value authenticity and meaningful conversations, central to any cultural exchange experience. Finally, I connected with mentors at study abroad organizations like Amigos de las Americas and the Stevens Initiative to help guide my thinking. This process led to the first iteration of Project Exchange's free, twelve-week online cultural exchange program.

The process of learning and better understanding the problem space happened *before* I started finding my people or selecting a tech platform. The best community builders have a robust understanding of why their community needs to exist, beyond the single instance that created the chip on their shoulder... so go find others experiencing a similar problem!

If you have thoughtful answers to both of the questions above, this book is your sign to take the leap and commit to community building. You have everything you need to get started. Alternatively, if you are not positioned to create something new, consider innovating within a pre-existing space. You can also think about who in your network does have the qualities of a good community builder. Just because you have a great idea doesn't mean you need to build it—consider sharing the idea with someone who can execute on it more effectively!

* * *

Hone Your Skills

Even if you fulfill the three minimum requirements, you might not feel 100 percent ready. Most of us haven't had many opportunities to practice digital-first community building skills. Maybe you've never been part of a flourishing community before, have never thought of yourself as a community builder, or are simply a bit nervous.

First, know you're not alone. Luckily, there's a good place for every new community builder to start: Serve as a community member!

Every great community builder has to start somewhere. Becoming an engaged member can help you understand what a flourishing community feels like, notice how the building blocks of community interact with each other, and practice community building skills through small experiments. Existing communities enable you to expand your knowledge of digital-first communities and what it takes to cultivate them, before committing time and energy to start your own.

It's helpful to point out perfectly designed communities that are 100 percent flourishing are incredibly rare. I, for one, can't say I've ever been in one… That said, communities can come close to flourishing and excel in certain areas. Each of the clubs, teams, and organizations you join is an opportunity to observe how different groups are applying community building concepts. Maybe you find a community especially talented in creating space through dialogue facilitation, but doesn't have great processes to empower new leaders. Maybe another community has a strong grasp of tech platforms, but no idea how to find their people. Instead of copying the entire framework of each community, reflect on what you like, don't like, and select specific practices you'd like to carry over!

Remember, structures and processes of healthy communities are designed to empower their members. They feature informal, evolving, and overlapping hierarchies built on passions and strengths, where even relatively new members can gain significant influence. Consequently, many community builders opt to gain experience by joining and assuming leadership roles in existing communities first.

Stepping into leadership opportunities can hone your community-building skills. Two strategies to lead include...

- **Volunteering**—Find ways to help, and if you don't know where to plug in, ask! Community builders want to invest in the community's hand raisers. Whether it's organizing break-out rooms at the next community call or providing feedback on a new cohort-based learning experience, you'll gain a behind-the-scenes look at how a digital community is run and nurture relationships with experienced community builders who may become helpful mentors later on.
- **Proposing and leading small experiments**—Lead experiments, especially the ones *you* want to see and would continue long-term if successful. The whole point of creating a new digital-first community is to address an unmet need. It's never too early to start identifying unmet needs and propose experiments that address them!

* * *

Apply Your Skills

Once you meet the minimum requirements of new community builders, understand the problem you're trying to solve, and grasp the practices of flourishing digital-first communities, you can move forward.

When done correctly, the transition from community member to community builder isn't too big a shift. What many people don't realize is in healthy communities, members are *already* builders. As mentioned above, you've had opportunities to identify problems and craft experiments to address them, whether it's a new ritual, updated community guidelines, or a new event series. As a community builder, you practice the same skills, just on a larger scale.

However, be aware of a few things during this transition. You'll need to…

- **Zoom out and take initiative**—Whereas members can decide to focus their time and energy on a small component of the community and trust everything else will move forward, community builders cannot do that. A larger chunk of your role is envisioning the big picture and identifying gaps, while also taking initiative to execute solutions.

- **Actively manage power asymmetries**—As the founder of the community, you'll find you're afforded higher status. In the beginning, you have relationships with most of your people. You'll likely know how to use the tech platform best, have the most informed perspective on community guidelines, and easily point to where every tiny piece of documentation is stored. With so much power, it's easy to slip into the dictator role and forget to co-create with members. It is up to you to take responsibility, acknowledge, and manage these asymmetries.

- **Pave what can be (at times) a lonely path**—Being a digital-first community builder is at times lonely, especially early in the journey. There's nothing quite like being the only person in your Zoom room, or people not taking your community seriously because you haven't accomplished anything yet. The important thing to remember is it won't always be this way! It might take some time for your community to find its stride, but with sustained attention and intention, it will.

Being a new community builder is no easy task, but one that is deeply rewarding. Communities can contribute to both your personal development and collective flourishing. This leads to the final step in the community building process: leverage your community for social change.

3.4

CHANGEMAKER

———

"But then the second thing he said was, 'You are inter-connected to everyone, because the world doesn't work without everyone.' You may think that you're alone, but you're never actually alone. This was really important because at a very young age that made me understand the importance of collectivity, and that we can't do anything alone that's worth it. Everything worthwhile is done with other people. So that became the soundtrack in my head."

—MARIAME KABA

One of the most important things I've realized while writing this book is community building *is* changemaking. Changemaking is love and respect in action. Everyone is valuable, everyone is powerful, and everyone is deserving of investment to realize their full potential. Community is the embodiment of that ideal.

For over a decade, Ashoka, an international nonprofit that launched the field of social entrepreneurship, has been building an "Everyone A Changemaker" world: a world in which every person steps up to solve problems for the greater good. They believe helping people see themselves as change-makers is more important than ever in a world defined by accelerating change, volatility, and hyperconnectivity.

The old world is one of repetitive efficiency (assembly lines and factories). Groups of people are organized into fixed hierarchies, siloed into distinct roles, tasked with transactional interactions to get things done, taught knowledge on a need-to-know basis, and given one set of skills to use day-in and day-out. In this paradigm, we forget we're all fundamentally interconnected. We lose our reverence for community; instead, our safety is in the money we make and material goods we own.

But that old story was written back in the 1700s, during the time of the Industrial Revolution. Technology has progressed since then. A new world and brighter future are possible if human consciousness progresses alongside innovation.

The good news is the new world is already emerging, and (surprise!) it is emerging in community.

This new world is defined by change and shared leadership. Instead of rigid command-and-control leadership, the new world features fluid, evolving hierarchies, distributed power, continuous learning, and collaboration built upon meaningful relationships. Trust is the default. It's something that is lost, not earned. As a result, everyone has the information they need to lead, and opportunities to grow into their full potential. Doesn't this remind you of the flourishing communities we described in Chapter 2.7: Empowering New Leaders?

In the new paradigm, we take time to get to know others who are different from us. We are open, authentic, and transparent—the truest expressions of ourselves. We remember all the ways the people around us have supported us.

The world is changing, and one of the simplest ways you can help the world navigate this change is by building communities that embody the new world. As Abraham Lincoln once said, "The best way to predict the future is to create it." If you're still waiting for a signal to start cultivating digital-first communities, observe the world around you. Look at the worsening "us-versus-them" politics spreading across the world. Notice the many injustices, from the disproportionate effects of climate change in the Global South to which Americans can and cannot vote. There are so many issues to tackle. These issues are worsened by the old-world paradigm, which makes transitioning to the new even more urgent.

Stop waiting for celebrities to use their platforms, corporations to take action, or politicians to get elected and "do the right thing." The truth is the vast majority of what can be done to better the world does not depend on the decisions people in power make. People are power. You give power, create power, and have power to build a brighter future.

While it might sound far-fetched, building the future starts with **you**. Here's why.

* * *

Building Power in People

Earlier, I mentioned how community building is really about power.

It is life-changing for people to articulate hopeful visions for the world, discover a community excited to build those visions with them, and realize they have the resources and support they need to get started. Instead of the world happening *to* them, the world is now something they shape with the people around them.

Community building allows us to rely less on traditional structures of power and become more self-sufficient and powerful on our own. We gain the ability to create the change we want to see.

In his book *You're More Powerful Than You Think*, co-founder and CEO of Citizen University Eric Liu describes how networks that empower its members to support each other with ideas, time, emotional support, and other resources put individuals in the power position. "Networks enable us to create exponential power from thin air: by setting off contagions of attitude and action, by activating every citizen as a potential node of transmission, and by creating global webs of knowledge and action," Liu writes.

Through repeated interactions in a safe space, community members build power through...

- **Emotional support**—At the most basic level, members in a flourishing community weave trust and develop intimacy by coming together over and over again. They get to know and care for people's souls, not just their roles. People realize they're not alone and many others share a similar vision for the future. Emotional support lays the groundwork for broad solidarity, like mutual care, inspiration, and acknowledgment.
- **Pooling and sharing resources**—Once emotional support is established, relationships bloom. People are able to communicate with each other well, which allows them to cultivate trust, deal with conflict, and manage power

dynamics. Community members start to develop shared reputation and accountability, which translates into more complex forms of solidarity beyond emotional support, like pooling together money. Sharing resources ensures every community member has what they need to flourish and move the collective forward.

- **Shared vision and responsibility**—Just like gardeners need a vision for the garden's maintenance and growth, community builders need to do the same for their people. Communities are not machines you can blame for "breaking." Liu explains "[communities] give their members the practice and experience of making *sure* things work. Which gives them more control over their own lives and outcomes." We start to realize community isn't something separate from us; it *is* us. Just like we have a responsibility over ourselves, we need to extend that to our communities.

- **Collective action**—Finally, with increased responsibility comes increased freedom to take real action. As Citizen University explains on Instagram, "When we notice something wrong, we dig in and get our hands dirty instead of sitting back and hoping things will get back on track. And when we nurture our garden when it's thriving, we're doing our part to make sure it's sustained and lives on." Whereas it's easy to neglect a backyard garden you're charged with developing on your own, it's much harder to do the same in the company of trusted friends you want to support.

In the past, these networks of people were only built in-person. We had limited autonomy around who we could get together with. Technology has broken down these barriers.

It is easier than ever to find folks who care about the same things and create change together. Beyond making it easy to discover, join, and onboard into communities relevant to our interests, digital-first communities are a low-pressure way to experience what building people power feels like at scale. The solidarity you feel from phone banking with folks located all over the U.S. is mind-blowing, especially when you don't have to physically go anywhere to find it!

* * *

Create Regenerative Space

Beyond streamlining change, digital communities also make change more sustainable.

When most people think of changemaking and Gen Z, they think of youth activism, things like climate strikes and March For Our Lives. What goes unsaid is many of these youth activist spaces are fueled by anger. Young people are called to speak truth to power, resist unjust systems, and hold adults and big corporations accountable. We're taught to take action solely *against* something, instead of imagining what a brighter future *could* be.

To be clear, activism is incredibly important in illuminating critical issues and emphasizing the *urgency* of these issues. Youth activism has been the catalytic force behind so much change.

However, while activism fueled by anger and resistance has the potential to unify and inspire in the short-term, it quickly burns out. A "shouting at everyone" lifestyle and constantly feeling like your future is being stolen is not sustainable. As a result, these spaces can become incredibly dis-empowering, toxic, and draining for the most engaged activists. Just think about it—we have so many youth activists but where are the civic superheroes? Why are people getting burned out? Why are they unable to engage in activism long term?

When youth activists struggle to find spaces where they are heard, when they aren't supported emotionally or with tangible resources, when their actions are constantly brushed aside, it becomes easy to believe activism is *supposed* to be draining.

Changemaking in digital-first community introduces a more sustainable form of activism inspired by belonging, mutual care, and love. It shows us activism and taking care of our communities isn't mutually exclusive with taking care of ourselves. Communities provide the critical social emotional support young changemakers need to make activism healing and inspiring.

As a community builder, you have a unique opportunity to help people experience this new form of changemaking. You can help people discover...

- **Support structures to take care of themselves**—The trust cultivated in communities enables members to pool together time, energy, and resources for community resilience, while giving each individual the freedom to contribute however they can. Instead of everyone doing everything themselves, communities encourage members to lean on each other for support, leverage each other's skill sets, and do things together that are impossible to do alone. People learn to consider their own needs because they can count on others.

- **Culture that promotes universal flourishing**—Culture is powerful because it consists of battle-tested processes and rituals proven to support the flourishing of individual members and the greater collective. Even if the resources and support structure for healing are present, people might not know how to fully utilize those resources without a culture that encourages it.
- **Participatory knowledge of what changemaking should feel like**—Beyond creating support structures and culture, communities offer spaces where people gather to *experience* joyful, meaningful changemaking. They encourage members to focus on what they can do and take action together. By providing optimism-generating things to talk about and build, communities help people unplug from anger-fueled changemaking and plug into love-fueled changemaking.

* * *

Your Time Is Now

Communities nurture more beautiful visions for the world and realize those visions on the smallest scales. Community builders get to do that with a like-minded group of friends who help us feel like we belong, are cared for, and have power to make a difference. Even if you don't see yourself as a changemaker yet or don't know what change you want to create, find and invest in communities that matter to you.

And while this chapter focused on the really big challenges communities are poised to tackle, it's important to emphasize no one community is more impactful than another. Whether you're reading this book to help your school's mental health club stay connected during the pandemic, to make your youth-led nonprofit more community-like, or to figure out how to strengthen the climate movement in your region, you're on the right path to generating meaningful change.

When you help people experience flourishing communities, you plant seeds of care, belonging, and power that create positive ripple effects in all sorts of friend groups, clubs, and organizations.

In Chapter 2.1: Two Provocations and the Canvas, I asked you to imagine a flourishing community, one where relationships flourish, everyone finds their you-shaped hole, people practice real power, and the community evolves on its own. I hope this book has shown you this type of community is attainable.

I'll leave you with one final note: Always remember that being a space maker and community builder is a joy practice. Don't take yourself too seriously and have fun! Being able to create the spaces we need and want to see is a privilege. It's truly amazing to see how much we're able to accomplish for ourselves and others. So don't squander the opportunities to create new communities. Help your existing groups become more community-spirited, or simply become a better community member.

You now have everything you need. Go forth and change the world!

ACKNOWLEDGEMENTS

Many people have helped make *Cultivate Community* possible. When I first started writing the book, I thought being an author was a solitary journey: I'd lock myself up in my room, write nonstop, and emerge three months later with a completed manuscript. What I have learned is that being an author is far from solitary. So many people have touched this book, whether it's by sharing their story, supporting my pre-sale campaign, hosting me on a podcast, serving as a beta reader, or even being part of a writing accountability group to keep me motivated. A book is not written alone, but rather written in community.

First and foremost, my deepest thanks go to my family: thank you to my parents, Doris and Roger, for supporting my dreams—no matter how unconventional they might be. Thank you to my two sisters, Jean and Joanne, for being my best friends and biggest cheerleaders. This book is certainly inspired by my childhood experiences. My mom is a bridge builder: I grew up watching her host potlucks that brought together people and communities who would've never met otherwise. My dad is a ritual designer: from Saturday family movie nights to Sunday mahjong, my dad has created structure that brings meaning and purpose into my life. My parents have challenged me to be both self-sufficient and form as many bonds as I can with others, knowing my world expands as I do.

This book would not have been written had I not discovered my love for digital-first community building through Civics Unplugged. In particular, I am grateful to Gary Sheng for responding to my Slack message about the Youth Organizers Collective in March 2020 and his mentorship since then. It's crazy to consider the upward spirals that a small experiment has sparked. I am grateful to the other good friends I have met through CU, especially those in Cool Cats and the Character-Virtue Crew. Thanks for showing me what beautiful online spaces feel like.

I have been blessed to be part of many flourishing communities (both online and in-person), where I have had opportunities to observe and experience the practices laid out in this book. These communities, including Project Exchange, TiE Young Entrepreneurs, Young Entrepreneurs Business Week, Girls Inc. of the Pacific Northwest, and the Riley's Way Foundation, have made bulk book pre-orders, allowed me to pilot workshops, and even tested the book in curriculum. These communities are brilliant and bring me incredible joy.

I am filled with gratitude every time I think about all the people who read early drafts of the book manuscript and offered insightful, kind, and challenging feedback. A special shout-out to my heavy pen readers—Madison Adams, Jean Lin,

Rachel Strauss, and Kristine Larson—who went through the manuscript and offered feedback (paragraph by paragraph in many instances). Madison helped sanity check **so many** ideas in this book and is an incredible thought partner. Jean challenged me to make this book more practically applicable for young leaders. Rachel restructured all of my sentences and forced me to be concise (an amazing feat). And Kristine contributed a wonderful flourishing lens that kept the book values-aligned. I have rewritten the book many times over thanks to their insights and provocations. I am also indebted to the other folks who have made their mark in the editing and revising early chapters: Eileen Dobzynski, Krystal Salmeron, Yubi Mamiya, Ash Kranti Srivastava, Tammy Pham, Nicole Chui, and Isabel Xue.

Thank you to the individuals that supported my pre-sale campaign:

Adam Schmierer, Afiya Williams, Alison Szopinski, Allie Magyar, Amanda Stuermer, Amanda Mitchell, Andrew Chen, Andrew Weiss, Ann-Marie Delgado, Ashlyn Nigh, Bettina Thompson, Cathy Cho, Celine Lin, Charlene Tanner, Chih Hsien Tu, Christine Liu, Christine O'Connell, D. Scott Smith, Dave Barcos, Denise Ellis, Devang Shah, Diana Hoff, Diane McClelland, Dominique Demetz, Donna Hansen, Eileen Dobzynski, Elizabeth Turner, Ella Murray, Elvia Santos Dominguez, Emily Yang, Eric Koester, Erin Aucar, Erin Bray, Erin Hamilton, Erin Jones, Evangeline Pattison, Fernanda Zabala, Gabriel Navarro, Gabrielle Bello, Gary Sheng, George Scarlett, Gracie Chick, Heather Wu, Hope Martinez, Huiling Chu, Ian Sandler, Isabel Xue, James Cantonwine, James Frohlich, Janice Jin, Jean Huang, Jean Lin,

Jessica Nielsen, Jie Zhao, Jill Jeske, Joan Huston, Joanne Yokoyama-Martin, Jodie Li, Josh Thompson, Julia Guo, Julia Terpak, Karen Ettinger, Kari Naone, Karl Keefer, Katherine Hanson, Katherine Sturdyvin-Scobba, Kathryn Joblon, Kathy Wang, Kelcey Burris, Kevin Connelly, Kevin Getch, Kevin Rabinovich, Kim Karr, Kody Richards, Laura Kikuchi, Lauren Shenkman, Laurie Albright, Lewis McMurran, Li Xu, Ling Fong, LouAnn Ross, Luna Abu-Yunis, Mackenzie Territo, Mariam Matin, Marjorie Hogan, Mark Burch, Mary Soplop, Maryam Tourk, Mikaela McCoy, Molly Wilson, Nick Woolf, Nicole Chui, Paul Cheung, Paul Edwards, Paul Warner, Rachel Ginocchio, Ruby Heidgerken, Russ Hedge, Ryan Cowden, Ryan Murphy, Sara duPont, Sara Fenton, Scott Judkins, Sean Mintz, Shane Gardner, Shashi Jain, Shu Ying Huang, Sophie Poole, Stephen Smolin, Tatiana Kolovou, Tie Xiao Wang, Tina Zhang, Therese Jornlin, Traci Johnson, Travis Cannon, Wendy Chang, Yu Chi, Yu-Fei Chou, Yu-Ping Kuan, Yubi Mamiya, Zaniya Lewis, Zhamilya Bilyalova, Zhan Chen.

It makes my heart full to see this group of mentors, teachers, and friends. This book wouldn't exist without your early support, and I'm so happy you're a part of this journey.

Last but not least, my deepest thanks to Eric Koester and the team at New Degree Press. I want to thank Karina Agbisit and Vivian Rose in particular—your energy, guidance, and resources were invaluable throughout the writing process. Thank you for challenging me to make the book the best it can be and offering support to help me get there.

There are no doubt people I have forgotten to mention. I am incredibly lucky to have so many inspirations and people who have made a difference in my life. To all of them, thank you. And thanks to you, reader, for giving your time to this book and embarking on the journey of cultivating digital-first communities. That is one of the greatest gifts you can give!

With love,
Ashley

APPENDIX

1.1 Definition of Community

Pfortmüller, Fabian. "What Does "Community" Even Mean? A Definition Attempt & Conversation Starter." *Together Institute* (blog). September 20, 2017. https://medium.com/together-institute/what-does-community-even-mean-a-definition-attempt-conversation-starter-9b443fc523do.

Merriam-Webster. s.v. "community (n.)." Accessed June 10, 2021. https://www.merriam-webster.com/dictionary/community.

1.2 Evolution of Digital Communities

Bromwich, Jonah. "How the Parkland Students Got So Good at Social Media." *New York Times*, March 7, 2018. https://www.nytimes.com/2018/03/07/us/parkland-students-social-media.html.

Chen, Richard. "The History of Internet Communities." *Richard Chen* (blog). January 16, 2019. https://rchen8.medium.com/the-history-of-internet-communities-f0234db848b1.

Cheung, Jane, Simon Glass, David McCarty, and Christopher Wong. *Generation Z: What brands should know about today's youngest consumers.* Somers, NY: Institute of Business Management Corporation, 2017.

Giles, Jim. "Internet Encyclopaedias Go Head to Head." *Nature* 438 (December 2005): 900-901. https://doi.org/10.1038/438900a.

Higgins, Josh. "The Evolution of Digital Communities and Where They're Headed." *Truss, Inc.* (blog). August 13, 2018. https://medium.com/@TrussInc/the-evolution-of-digital-communities-and-where-theyre-headed-65afbo3acbb.

Mander, Jason, Chase Buckle, and Thomas Morris. *Gen Z: Observing the latest trends on Gen Zs.* GlobalWebIndex, 2020.

Pew Research Center. "Experts Predict More Digital Innovation by 2030 Aimed at Enhancing Democracy." Internet. Updated June 30, 2020. https://www.pewresearch.org/internet/2020/06/30/innovations-these-experts-predict-by-2030/.

RadiumOne. *The Light and Dark of Social Sharing: Harnessing the power of consumer connections.* RadiumOne, 2014.

Rosenblatt, Kalhan. "Despite a Sense of Hopelessness, March For Our Lives Urges Young People to Vote." *NBC News*, August 21, 2020. https://www.nbcnews.com/news/us-news/despite-sense-hopelessness-march-our-lives-urges-young-people-vote-n1237534.

Strickler, Yancey. "The Dark Forest Theory of the Internet (Ideaspace #16)." *The Ideaspace* (blog). May 16, 2019. https://ideaspace.substack.com/p/the-dark-forest-theory-of-the-internet.

Tapatalk. *Tapatalk: Study Finds Americans Trust Specialized Forums Over Facebook.* Tapatalk, 2019.

Wilson, Sara. "The Era of Antisocial Social Media." *Harvard Business Review*, February 5, 2020. https://hbr.org/2020/02/the-era-of-antisocial-social-media.

Zuckerman, Ethan. "A History of Digital Communities... In Seven Minutes." *Ethan Zuckerman* (blog). May 12, 2006. https://ethanzuckerman.com/2006/05/12/a-history-of-digital-communities-in-seven-minutes/.

1.3 Why Now: Benefits and Trends

Calma, Justine. "A 72-Hour Livestream Is Bringing Earth Day Online: The 50th anniversary of Earth Day marks a new chapter of digital resistance." *The Verge*, April 21, 2020. https://www.theverge.com/2020/4/21/21229975/earth-day-50th-anniversary-live-stream.

Cigna. *Cigna 2018 US Loneliness Index*. Cigna, 2018.

The Institute of Museum and Library Services. *Public Libraries in the United States: Fiscal year 2017, Volume II*. The Institute of Museum and Library Services, 2020.

Jones, Jeffrey. "US Church Membership Falls Below Majority for First Time." *Gallup*, March 29, 2021. https://news.gallup.com/poll/341963/church-membership-falls-below-majority-first-time.aspx.

Klinenberg, Eric. *Palaces for the People: How Social Infrastructure Can Help Fight Inequality, Polarization, and the Decline of Civic Life*. New York: Penguin Random House LLC, 2018.

Nelson, Mick. *USA Swimming—Facilities Development*. USA Swimming, 2013.

Nierenberg, Amelia, and Tristan Spinsky. "New Spirits Rise in Old, Repurposed Churches." *New York Times*, October 25, 2020.

https://www.nytimes.com/2020/10/25/us/abandoned-churches-covid.html.

Putnam, Robert. "Bowling Alone: America's Declining Social Capital." *Journal of Democracy* 6, no. 1 (January 1995): 65-78. http://doi.org/10.1353/jod.1995.0002.

Roser, Max, Hannah Ritchie, and Esteban Ortiz-Ospina. "Internet." *Our World in Data.* 2015. https://ourworldindata.org/internet.

Vaughan, Sophie. "The Sunrise Movement's Phone Banking Operation Is a Force for Change." *Teen Vogue*, July 14, 2020. https://www.teenvogue.com/story/sunrise-movement-phonebanking.

2.1 Two Provocations, A Metaphor, And the Canvas

Pfortmüller, Fabian, Nico Luchsinger, and Sascha Mombartz. "Community Canvas." Accessed June 13, 2021. https://community-canvas.org/.

2.2 Find Your People

Gibbons, Serenity. "You And Your Business Have 7 Seconds to Make A First Impression: Here's How to Succeed." *Time*, June 19, 2018. https://www.forbes.com/sites/serenitygibbons/2018/06/19/you-have-7-seconds-to-make-a-first-impression-heres-how-to-succeed/?sh=3364eebc56c2.

New_ Public. "Tend to Your Digital Gardens: Flowers, Weeds, and All." *New_Public* (blog). June 13, 2021. https://newpublic.substack.com/p/-tend-to-your-digital-gardens-flowers.

2.3 Technology

Frank, Allegra. "AOC Met More Than 400,000 Young Potential Voters on Their Own Turf: Twitch." *Vox*, October 22, 2020. https://www.vox.com/2020/10/22/21526625/aoc-twitch-stream-among-us-most-popular-twitch-streams-ever.

Schroeder, Juliana, Michael Kardas, and Nicholas Epley. "The Humanizing Voice: Speech Reveals, and Text Conceals, a More Thoughtful Mind in the Midst of Disagreement." *Psychological Science* 28, no. 12 (Winter 2017): 1745-1762. https://doi.org/10.1177%2F0956797617713798.

2.4 Create Space

Brown, Jessica, Louie Montoya, and Sam Seidel. "Setting Group Intentions for Brave Spaces." Stanford d.school. Accessed June 15, 2021. https://dschool.stanford.edu/resources/norms.

2.5 Facilitate Transformation

Brown, Brené. *Braving the Wilderness: The Quest for True Belonging and the Courage to Stand Alone*. New York: Penguin Random House LLC, 2017.

Forte, Tiago. "The Future of Education is Community: The Rise of Cohort-Based Courses." *Forte Labs* (blog). March 8, 2021. https://fortelabs.co/blog/the-rise-of-cohort-based-courses/.

Forte, Tiago. "The Future of Online Learning: STEVEs (Short Tiny Exclusive Virtual Experiences)." *Forte Labs* (blog). February 19, 2017. https://fortelabs.co/blog/the-future-of-online-learning-steves-short-tiny-exclusive-virtual-experiences/.

Ozenc, Kursat. "Introducing Ritual Design: Meaning, Purpose, and Behavior Change." *Ritual Design Lab* (blog). April 1, 2016. https://medium.com/ritual-design/introducing-ritual-design-meaning-purpose-and-behavior-change-44d26d484edf#.2ktdz2fct.

Parker, Priya. *The Art of Gathering: How We Meet and Why It Matters*. New York: Riverhead Books, 2018.

Reich, Justin, and José A. Ruipérez-Valiente. "The MOOC Pivot." *Science* 363, no. 6423 (January 2019): 130-131. https://doi.org/10.1126/science.aav7958.

ter Kuile, Casper. *The Power of Ritual: Turning Everyday Activities into Soulful Practices*. New York: HarperOne, 2020.

2.6 Establish Your Vibe

Agrawal, Radha. *Belong: Find Your People, Create Community, and Live a More Connected Life*. New York: Workman Publishing Company, 2018.

Chayka, Kyle. "TikTok and the Vibes Revival." *The New Yorker*, April 2021.

Closing the Loop. "Tiktok, Emergent Creativity, The Limits of Social Graphs, and whatever else Eugene talked about (E1)." May 21, 2021. Video, 1:25:54. https://youtu.be/xbnDay35L8I.

Morse, John, and Jay Lorsch. "Beyond Theory Y." *Harvard Business Review*, May 1970.

National Geographic Society. "Storytelling and Cultural Traditions." Resource Library. Updated January 24, 2020. https://www.nationalgeographic.org/article/storytelling-and-cultural-traditions/.

Working Narratives. "What is Public Narrative and How Can We
Use It?" *Working Narratives* (blog). Accessed June 18, 2021.
https://workingnarratives.org/article/public-narrative/.

2.7 Empower New Leaders

Cabraal, Anthony, and Susan Basterfield. *Better Work Together:
How the Power of Community Can Transform Your Business.*
New Zealand: Enspiral Foundation, 2018.

Doyle, Glennon. *Untamed.* New York: The Dial Press, 2020.

Elise, Margot. "Meet Naj Austin, Founder of the First Social
and Wellness Club for People of Color." *Jopwell*, February 12,
2020. https://www.jopwell.com/thewell/posts/meet-naj-austin-
founder-of-the-first-social-and-wellness-club-for-people-of.

Fung, Katherine. "Shopify CEO Sends Email to Staff Saying Company Is 'Not a Family': 'We Cannot Solve Every Societal Problem'." *Newsweek*, May 18, 2021. https://www.newsweek.com/
shopify-ceo-sends-email-staff-saying-company-not-family-
we-cannot-solve-every-societal-1592545.

Gawande, Atul. *The Checklist Manifesto: How to Get Things Right.*
New York: Picador, 2010.

Hamel, Gary, and Michele Zanini. *Humanocracy: Creating Organizations as Amazing as the People Inside Them.* Boston: Harvard
Business Review Press, 2020.

3.1 Qualities of a Good Community Builder

Alexander, Franz. "Emotional Maturity." Address delivered at
the Institute on Nursing Education, Chicago, IL, November

1948. https://repositories.lib.utexas.edu/bitstream/handle/
2152/20488/txu-oclc-2741165.pdf?sequence=2.
McCauley, Dana. "Why intelligence, talent and charisma are vastly
overrated." *New York Post*, June 9, 2016. https://nypost.com/
2016/06/09/why-intelligence-talent-and-charisma-are-vastly-
overrated/.

3.2 Culture Changer

Zaraska, Marta. "Moving in Sync Creates Surprising Social Bonds
Among People." *Scientific American*, October 1, 2020.
https://www.scientificamerican.com/article/moving-in-sync-
creates-surprising-social-bonds-among-people/.

3.4 Changemaker

Citizen University. "Just like a garden, democracy takes effort, care,
and work to thrive. Living like a citizen in our democracy
means we have to think and act like a gardener." *Instagram*.
September 24, 2020.
https://www.instagram.com/p/CFhpYK6AgS8/.
Drayton, Bill. "The New Reality." *Ashoka Key Ideas* (blog). February 1, 2019. https://www.ashoka.org/en-in/story/new-reality.
Liu, Eric. *You're More Powerful Than You Think: A Citizen's Guide
to Making Change Happen*. New York: PublicAffairs, 2017.

Made in the USA
Columbia, SC
22 April 2023